MW00790506

NATIVE TEXAN

★ STORIES FROM DEEP IN THE HEART ★

JOE HOLLEY

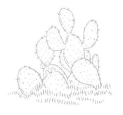

MAVERICK BOOKS / TRINITY UNIVERSITY PRESS
SAN ANTONIO

Published by Maverick Books, an imprint of Trinity University Press
San Antonio, Texas 78212

The stories that appear here were originally published in the *Houston Chronicle* and are reprinted courtesy of Hearst.

Book design by Anne Richmond Boston
Illustrations by Kate Holley
Author photo by Mark Burns

978-1-59534-945-3 PAPER
978-1-59534-309-3 EBOOK

Trinity University Press strives to produce its books using methods and materials in an environmentally sensitive manner. We favor working with manufacturers that practice sustainable management of all natural resources, produce paper using recycled stock, and manage forests with the best possible practices for people, biodiversity, and sustainability. The press is a member of the Green Press Initiative, a nonprofit program dedicated to supporting publishers in their efforts to reduce their impacts on endangered forests, climate change, and forest-dependent communities.

The paper used in this publication meets the minimum requirements of the American National Standard for Information Sciences—Permanence of Paper for Printed Library Materials, ANSI 39.48–1992.

CIP data on file at the Library of Congress

28 27 26 25 24 | 5 4 3 2 1

To Laura

And in memory of my mother, Mildred Moore Holley,
valedictorian of Bigfoot High School, Class of 1932

CONTENTS

INTRODUCTION

A mong my various duties as a staff writer at the *Washington Post*, I often wrote obituaries. The *Post*, along with the *New York Times* and *Los Angeles Times*, was among the few newspapers that still took obituaries seriously, treating them as legitimate news stories, minibiographies of people whose lives made a difference. During my time there I wrote obits of prominent politicians, artists, entertainers, athletes, and business figures as well as crooks and common folks. I especially enjoyed writing about the latter, whose unsung lives often were just as fascinating as those we were accustomed to seeing in the media. It's just that no one had thought to ask about them until they had passed on.

Meanwhile, I also carved out an unofficial beat at the *Post*: writing profiles of eccentric, unusual, or outrageous Texans. "Gee, Mr. Holley, you sure must be busy!" one of my journalism students at George Washington University observed. Youngster that she was, she assumed that every Texan was eccentric, unusual, or outrageous. (I can't imagine where she got the idea.)

My two beats coalesced on a January day in 2006 when I suggested to my editor that we note the passing of one Juanita Dale Slusher, an Edna native better known among Texans of a certain age as Candy Barr. (Ms. Slusher had a yen for Snickers, thus the name.) Considered "the first porn star" because of her appearance at age sixteen in an early underground pornographic film, she was a hit at strip clubs in downtown Dallas in the pre-MeToo era of the 1950s and '60s. Her close friend was Jack Ruby, the Dallas club owner who shot and killed Lee Harvey Oswald on live TV two days after the assassination of John F. Kennedy. She and Ruby shared an affection for dachshunds.

Barr, who had been abused as a child, was notorious for her nightly performance at the Colony Club in downtown Dallas, a few blocks from city hall. As I wrote in the *Post*, "Big-spending businessmen, conventioneers out on the town, local politicos, cops and hustlers, not to mention wide-eyed country boys from Canton or Waxahachie all crowded into the club to ogle the blond beauty."

The morning the Barr obit appeared, *Post* owner Don Graham stopped by my desk in the newsroom. He had a big grin on his face. "Joe," he asked, "how well *did* you know that woman?"

Graham's sly compliment was a reminder to me that when I wrote about Texas and my fellow Texans, I wrote with more verve and authority. I knew Texas in ways I would never know anywhere else.

I identified with the late Willie Morris, my eminent predecessor by a couple of decades as editor of the *Texas Observer*. Morris once wrote, "As if in a dream, where every gesture is attenuated, it grew upon me that a man had best be coming back to where his strongest feelings lay. For there, then, after all of it, was the heart."

For Morris, that place was Mississippi; for me, it was Texas. I liked living in D.C., but when I got the opportunity I headed home to write about the place I couldn't shake, the place that was in my blood, in my heart.

Some years ago, my friend and fellow Waco native Lyndon Olson, living in New York City at the time, was flying out of La Guardia Airport, on his way to Waco. President Bill Clinton had just appointed Lyndon ambassador to Sweden, and this would be his last Texas visit before taking up his post in Stockholm. A ticket agent happened to notice his destination.

"Waco!" the agent exclaimed (with a smirk, no doubt). "Why would anybody want to go to Waco?"

Keep in mind that the Branch Davidian siege had come to its horrific end a few years earlier, so people who knew little if anything about our hometown knew its connection to that tragedy. Waco's reputation was on the downside, to be sure (even though, as my Aunt Gaynell, a longtime Wacoan, forcefully reminded non-Texans, the Branch Davidian compound wasn't even in Waco; it was in nearby Elk).

My answer to the airport skeptic would have been similar to Lyndon's: Waco is home. Waco is family. And so is Texas.

Texas is the place we know and care about, a place we cannot scrub off our soul (to paraphrase the late Texas writer A. C. Greene), even when we have our differences and disagreements, even when it drives us crazy. Like family. (Lyndon, by the way, came home to Waco after his diplomatic stint.)

The Native Texan columns collected here originally appeared in the *Houston Chronicle*. They are about people, about places, about the past. The ones I like the best are about all three.

I confess to writing the occasional column about Waco—whose reputation has revived spectacularly thanks in large part to an attractive young couple whose cable TV show about fixing up Waco-area houses is a nationwide phenomenon—but mainly I write about towns small and large across the state that happen to strike my fancy. Readers suggest ideas or I'll happen to read about a place or a moment in history, a moment that may have been ignored by the history books, and I'll hop in the car and go investigate. (It's a good gig, to be sure.) Or, without a particular topic, I'll claim a table at the Dairy Queen in a little town like Henderson or Archer City—Larry McMurtry's Archer City—and likely come away with a tale worth telling. That's Texas.

I'm not necessarily interested in tourist attractions or the best barbecue joint in town—although, in the tradition of investigative journalism, I'm happy to give the ribs and brisket a try. I'm interested primarily in the people who've made Texas home, in their ties to the land and to their neighbors. I'm interested in the personality, the particularity of a place, whether it's a burgeoning metropolis like Dallas or Houston or a little town like Mexia (pronounced Muh-HAY-Uh) or Tivoli (pronounced Tuh-VO-Li). I'm interested in memory and how the past lives on, continuing to shape and mold the present.

I want my fellow Texans to know, for example, about Black Seminoles who settled in the Trans-Pecos; about a young man from Fayetteville named John C. C. Hill, who held off a Mexican army; about Robert Howard, a young man from Cross Plains who created an iconic action hero that Arnold Schwarzenegger brought to life on the big screen. And I beg the reader's indulgence to tell a few family stories—one, for example, about Uncle Joe, my namesake, and his encounter with Bonnie and Clyde's driver Raymond Hamilton in a Hillsboro jail cell. (Joe survived and prospered; Hamilton met his demise in the electric chair.)

My hope, dear reader, is that you enjoy these stories and others in this book as much as I enjoyed teasing them out of this wonderfully intriguing place we call Texas. Always and everywhere in Texas, there are stories worth telling.

Texans Who Dropped Out of the History Books
(or Were Never There to Begin With)

Thinking about these places, and the generations of people who lived in them . . . reminds me that the story of Texas has always played out beneath and beyond the canopy of Big History.

— STEPHEN HARRIGAN,
Big Wonderful Thing: A History of Texas

THE INCREDIBLE SAGA OF JOHN C. C. HILL
FAYETTEVILLE

I t's the day after Christmas, 1842. In the Mexican border town of Mier, downriver from Nuevo Laredo, a citizen soldier from Fayette County, Texas, stands before his captor, Mexican general Pedro de Ampudia. The soldier, John Christopher Columbus Hill, is part of the Somervell Expedition, an ill-conceived effort to invade Mexico and put an end once and for all to Mexican adventurism in the Republic of Texas. After a bloody engagement with Mexican forces that began on Christmas day, the outmanned Texans have been forced to surrender.

Ampudia has commandeered the comfortable home of the Mier alcalde as his headquarters. Hill, hat in hand, is escorted into the main room of the house. His clothes and shoes ragged, his face gaunt, he's well aware that Ampudia may order his execution, particularly when he responds truthfully to the general's interrogation about his actions during the fierce fighting. Tears have traced white lines down cheeks blackened by dirt and gunpowder.

"I can count twelve of your men, and it may have been fifteen that I picked off," Hill admits, "but I am not sure of but twelve." Mexican soldiers in the room confirm his account. Each man had been shot in the head, they report. The Texan has one other bit of information for the general: He has just turned fourteen.

Although passing references to the remarkable John C. C. Hill pop up through the years, the only book-length treatment I've seen is a young adult biography by Mary Margaret McAllen Amberson of San Antonio, *A Brave Boy and a Good Soldier: John C. C. Hill and the Texas Expedition to Mier*. The dialogue I quote is from her account, published in 2006.

Young Hill's adventure began in September 1842 on the family farm near Fayetteville. He and his pals were standing around in the yard playing mumblety-peg, the old game that involves flipping a pocketknife into the ground, the winner being the one who can plant the knife closest to his bare feet without stabbing himself. Inside the house, his father, Asa, and an older brother, Jeffrey, were preparing to ride to San Antonio with other volunteers to join up with a company under the command of Gen. Alexander Somervell. Mexican forces under Gen. Adrian Woll had recently seized the city.

John Hill folded his knife, marched into the house, and announced that he was going too. His parents, his brother Jeffrey, and another older brother, James Monroe Hill, looked down at the slight, fresh-faced thirteen-year-old and told him that was ridiculous. Although the boy reminded them that he had made it to Austin and back on family business a few months earlier, his mother, Elizabeth, was adamant. "Asa, he is so delicate looking," she said. "It's as bad as taking one of the girls."

Her argument backfired. Asa concluded that the experience would toughen up the boy and equip him for the hardships of frontier life. After a long night of prayer, Elizabeth gave in.

Just as the Hills were leaving, older brother James, unable to go because of ill health, handed John the muzzle-loading flintlock he had used at the Battle of San Jacinto. Never let it fall into the hands of the enemy, he told his little brother.

John mounted his pony, Jim Dandy. As the party headed down the trail toward Seguin, he turned and waved to his mother, sisters, and brother. "I shall never see him again," Elizabeth Hill said.

The militia members, quarrelsome and undisciplined, numbered close to a thousand as they headed toward the border. By the time they got to Laredo on December 7, several hundred had decided they had more pressing matters to attend to back home. When serious fighting broke out in the streets and on the rooftops of Mier two weeks later, the Texans were up against a force of more than two thousand men.

A commanding officer assigned Hill to a niche atop the roof of a building where he could see the Mexican army's cannon without being seen. Relying on shooting skills he'd honed back home, the boy picked off artillerymen each time they raised their heads. As he told the general, he killed at least a dozen men.

The battle lasted twenty-three hours. Despite being heavily outnumbered, the Texans were winning without realizing it. Exhausted, running out of ammunition, and hearing rumors of Mexican reinforcements on the way, they decided to surrender. Rounded up in the town plaza, they were ordered to toss their weapons onto a pile. Young Hill refused. Remembering his brother's admonition, he broke his rifle apart on paving stones.

Ampudia, whose own adopted son had died an agonizing death a few hours earlier in the room of the house where he questioned Hill, was intrigued by the young Texan. Instead of ordering his execution or throwing him into a cramped jail cell with his father and brother and their comrades, he was fed, allowed to take a bath, and given new clothes. He stayed in the alcalde's comfortable home.

Ampudia wanted to adopt the boy, but Antonio López de Santa Anna, president of the Republic of Mexico, had first dibs. He had the boy escorted to the presidential palace in Mexico City and proposed not only adoption but also enrollment in an officer's training school at the military academy located in the historic Chapultepec Castle. Hill turned him down, telling the president he was Texan by birth and intended to remain so. "Our prisoner dictates terms," an amused Santa Anna remarked to an aide.

Meanwhile, the boy's fellow Texans, including his father and brother, were being marched toward Mexico City, seven hundred miles away. Manacled in pairs, they struggled under heavy guard over rocky hills, the only shade from spindly mesquite and prickly pear. Starving, nearly naked, some without shoes, a number died during the three-month ordeal.

On March 13, 1843, their captors paused at a place called Salado to hear a new decree from the one-legged Mexican president: Every tenth man would be executed, the victims chosen by lottery. Seventeen men who reached their hand into an earthen jar and drew a black bean instead of white were lined up against a wall and shot by firing squad. Those who survived the forced march ended up in a cold, dank prison between Mexico City and Vera Cruz called Perote. Imprisoned for two years under inhumane conditions, most made it back to Texas, Asa Hill and son Jeffrey among them.

John Hill, by then known as Juan Cristobal Colombo Gil, stayed in Mexico. Living with a foster family Santa Anna had picked for him, he received his doctorate in engineering from the prestigious Colegio de Minería and became an esteemed civil engineer. In years to come, he would supervise mining operations and lay out a number of Mexico's railroad lines. During the Mexican War, he got to know Ulysses S. Grant and helped as an interpreter while the Treaty of Guadalupe Hidalgo was being negotiated. He also became a physician who practiced holistic medicine. He and his wife, Augustina, sister of the famous Mexican painter Ramón Sagredo, were the parents of four children.

In 1855, more than a dozen years after leaving the family farm on the back of Jim Dandy, John Christopher Columbus Hill returned to Texas for a visit. Asa Hill had died a few years earlier. Standing on her front porch, a tearful Elizabeth Hill watched the self-assured young man walking toward her, his arms outstretched, a smile creasing his handsome face. She must have found it hard to believe that this was the son who had left so long ago, the son she thought she would never see again.

ROBERT NEIGHBORS SOUGHT TO BLAZE A PATH OF PEACE

FORT BELKNAP

During my time in D.C. a few years ago, I spent a day at the Library of Congress trying to confirm a Texas tale that had long intrigued me. It involved a man named Robert Simpson Neighbors, a frontiersman well known among Texas historians but not that well known generally. A Virginian who got to Texas in 1836 at age twenty, a friend of Sam Houston's, Neighbors was a big, red-haired fellow whose belief in the basic humanity of Native Americans cost him his life. A genuine Texas hero, he ought to have streets and counties named after him instead of being a mere historical footnote.

The Neighbors story that prompted my library search is in *Lambshead before Interwoven: A Texas Range Chronicle*, a 1982 history of early settlements in northwest Texas by the late Frances Mayhugh Holden of Lubbock. Neighbors, working as a federal Indian agent in the mid-1840s, was trying to persuade various Texas tribes to, in Houston's words, "walk the path of peace" and retreat to newly established "reserves." He had learned to speak Comanche and had earned the tribes' trust.

In 1846, according to Holden, Neighbors escorted a group of Indian leaders, including Santa Anna and Old Owl of the Comanches and José María of the Anadarkos, on a visit to Washington. The party rode the fifteen hundred miles on horseback.

The purpose of the visit was to expose the chiefs to the power and wealth of the United States and demonstrate what they were up against if they continued to resist the relentless wave of white settlement. They stayed in the nation's capital for a month.

Imagine that scene—self-possessed Indian leaders riding their horses along loud and busy Pennsylvania Avenue, the thoroughfare lined with buildings and crowded with carriages, buggies, horses, and people. Imagine these dark-skinned men in their tribal regalia walking through the majestic Capitol, meeting with Houston in the marble halls of the Senate. The larger-than-life Texan no doubt was wearing his own Indian regalia when he welcomed the delegation. Neighbors stayed in the Globe Hotel but found a place for the chiefs "in the suburbs." The noise and bustle of downtown D.C. disturbed them.

Neither I nor a couple of Library of Congress librarians who also got interested in the chiefs' visit could find any documentation, but, of course, that doesn't mean it didn't happen. Holden's source was apparently the late Kenneth Neighbours, a historian at Midwestern State University in Wichita Falls and the author of the definitive Neighbors biography.

"If Neighbours wrote it, you could take it to the bank," Ty Cashion, a historian at Sam Houston State University, told me.

However awed and impressed the chiefs were by Washington, D.C., a number of tribes in the early 1850s did agree, reluctantly, to move onto three reservations established in northwest Texas, two known collectively as the Brazos Reservation near present-day Graham and the third, called the Clear Fork Reservation, in Throckmorton and Shackelford Counties. Several smaller tribes settled on the Brazos Reservation in 1855, while three sizable Comanche bands—"skittish, aloof and skeptical," Holden writes—arrived shortly afterward.

Two years later the *Houston Republic* printed the following: "From Major Neighbors we learn that there are now in the 'reserve' in Texas about 1500 Indians. . . . The Indians cultivate the soil, and have made a good crop this year. . . . They also learn to work at the blacksmith's trade. The people live very near to each other, and appear to be weaned from their roving life."

Neighbors, who in Cashion's words "appreciated the First Nations on their own terms, which most people did not," soon realized that "their roving life" was not the problem. His most urgent challenge was protecting the Indians from white settlers who wanted them eradicated and annihilated. Renegade whites inspired by Indian agent and former Texas legislator John R. Baylor—"a rabble-rouser of the first order," in Holden's words—worked to undercut Neighbors, by then a federal Indian superintendent for the Texas tribes. Agitators across North Texas stole Indian horses and cattle. They murdered both white men and Natives while masquerading as Indians.

Vowing to destroy the Indians in revenge for their depredations, Baylor raised an "army" of about 250 farmers and stockmen and attacked the Brazos Reservation. His motley group killed an old man and scalped him before being driven off by federal troops and the Indians themselves. Baylor lost five of his men.

It wasn't just the renegades who resented Neighbors's efforts. He was "immensely courageous," historian T. R. Fehrenbach has written, but he "was more successful at winning friends and influencing people among the Indians than in getting the cooperation or sympathy of his own kind."

In spring 1857 Neighbors and his wife, Elizabeth Ann, journeyed to Washington to confer with President James Buchanan and Sen. Sam Houston about moving the Texas Indians into Indian

Territory (Oklahoma) for their own protection. He received the permission he sought in 1859.

Early on the morning of August 1, Neighbors set in motion an exodus of more than 1,400 Indians, under military escort and accompanied by carts, wagons, cattle, oxen, mules, horses, and dogs. In the shimmering heat of summer, the strange cavalcade, at once magnificent and sad, stretched across the prairie for nearly three miles.

Neighbors wrote to his wife about the departure: "If you want to hear a full description of our Exodus out of Texas, read the 'Bible' where the children of Israel crossed the Red Sea. We have had about the same show, only our enemies did not follow us to the Red River. If they had—the Indians would have in all probability sent them back without the interposition of Divine Providence."

The combined tribes arrived at the Red River on August 8. Neighbors and the military escort accompanied them for another seven days until they reached the valley of the Washita River, a place Neighbors described as "truly a splendid country," with excellent grass and good water. Bidding the Indians farewell, one by one, he left for Texas on September 6.

On the morning of September 14, Neighbors stopped at Belknap, in Young County, to write up his report. As he stepped out of the courthouse a couple of hours later, a man named Edward Cornett emerged from behind a chimney and shot him in the back.

Neighbors, forty-three, died on the street, the local sheriff cradling his head. His killer, known as a "drinking, blustering, dissolute desperado," was a Baylor sympathizer. He was never arrested, although a band of Texas Rangers administered their own brand of justice months after the murder.

BASS REEVES, THE GREATEST FRONTIERSMAN IN AMERICAN HISTORY

PARIS

Wandering into the stately Lamar County courthouse one morning not long ago, I asked the sheriff's deputy manning the metal detector where in the building I could find Bass Reeves. He didn't know, even though Reeves was a fellow lawman and, like the deputy, had Paris connections.

As it turned out, the man who may have been the model for the Lone Ranger and who may be on the verge of a turn in the spotlight rivaling Disney's Davy Crockett was upstairs. Installed on a stairway landing in the form of a small statue was a formidable-looking African American man in boots, duster, and western hat, cigar clenched in his teeth, a badge attached to his coat, double-barreled shotgun at the ready.

Created by Eddie Dixon, a Lubbock-based sculptor known for his renderings of iconic African Americans, the Reeves work has been in the courthouse since being donated by a local benefactor in 2010.

Bass Reeves, for now, is not a household name, although among frontier-history aficionados he's the one Black lawman everybody knows. For good reason. As his biographer, Art T. Burton, told me by phone from his home near Chicago, "He's the greatest frontiersman in American history. He was a phenomenon."

He was born in July 1838—near Paris, according to the *Handbook of Texas*, although Burton maintains he was born near Van Buren, Arkansas. As Burton tells the story in *Black Gun, Silver Star: The Life and Legend of Frontier Marshal Bass Reeves,* Bass and his family—bearing the surname of their enslaver—were owned by William Steele Reeves, originally from Tennessee. When the youngster was eight, the Reeves family and its slaves moved to North Texas as part of the Peters Colony, an empresario grant founded by twenty English and American investors in Grayson County, just south of the Red River. Burton, a retired college history professor, mentioned that William S. Reeves just may have been Bass Reeves's father.

At some point after the move to Texas, Bass became something of a bodyguard, valet, and companion to William Reeves's son, George Reeves, who would go on to serve as Grayson County's tax collector and then sheriff before being elected to the Texas House in 1855. Bass Reeves was always in his company. At the outbreak of the Civil War, George Reeves was made a colonel in the 11th Texas Cavalry Regiment. Bass Reeves rode into battle with him as the regiment took part in the Battle of Chustenahlah in Indian Territory, the Battle of Pea Ridge in Arkansas, and other engagements.

After the war, George Reeves—for whom Reeves County is named—would win reelection to the Texas House, eventually becoming speaker. He died of hydrophobia in 1882 after being bitten by a rabid dog.

George Reeves and Bass Reeves had parted years earlier, and not only because Bass had been freed by the Emancipation Proclamation. During the war, the two young men were playing cards and got into an argument. Burton, quoting Bass's youngest daughter, wrote that Bass "laid him out cold with his fist and then made a run for Indian Territory."

Seminole and Creek Indians, always hospitable to runaway slaves, took him in. He learned their languages, honed his already formidable shooting skills, and became a superb horseman. According to Burton, he also perfected techniques of disguise and stealth in combat.

No longer a fugitive after the war, Bass left Indian Territory and settled near Van Buren, becoming a stockman and farmer. He married Nellie Jennie (or Jenney), a Texan, and the couple had ten children, five boys and five girls. After the death of his wife, Reeves married Winnie Sumter of Muskogee, Oklahoma, and started a second family.

Occasionally serving as a scout for deputy U.S. marshals venturing into Indian Territory, Reeves himself was commissioned as a deputy U.S. marshal in 1875. According to Burton, he wasn't the first African American deputy marshal west of the Mississippi, but he soon became the best known. At six feet, two inches tall and 190 pounds, he not only cut a formidable figure but also developed a reputation as a tough, resourceful, and relentless lawman. Working alongside mostly white U.S. marshals on the trail of outlaws who had taken refuge in Indian Territory, he was a sharpshooter familiar with the land and languages. The tribes, always wary of whites, knew and trusted the Black lawman.

Working out of Fort Smith under Judge Isaac Parker, the famous "hanging judge" presiding over the U.S. District Court for the Western District of Arkansas, he headed into Indian Territory on the trail of fugitives—Black, Native American, and white—who assumed they were beyond the reach of both federal and tribal law. Often he returned with more than a dozen outlaws in custody. Reeves himself said he once brought in nineteen horse thieves operating in the Fort Sill area of what is today Oklahoma.

Christian Wallace, writing about Reeves in *Texas Monthly* a couple of years ago, had this to say about his reputation: "Some criminals were so afraid of Reeves they turned themselves in as soon as they heard he was after them. He stalked others in their nightmares. Once, Reeves even arrested his own son for murder."

"He is six feet tall, sixty-eight years old, and looks to be forty," the *Fort Smith Times* wrote in 1907. "He was never known to show the slightest excitement under any circumstance. He does not know what fear is, and to him, the supreme document and law of the country is a 'writ.' Place a warrant for arrest in his hands and no circumstance can cause him to deviate."

Burton credits Reeves with having arrested more than three thousand fugitives during his thirty-two-year career as a marshal in Fort Smith, Paris, and Sherman. He not only relied on his prowess with a gun but occasionally disguised himself to apprehend the unsuspecting. One among numerous Reeves tales that blend into legend has him trudging along the trail for nearly thirty miles dressed as a beggar on the run from the law. Arriving at the home of his targets, two brothers hiding out in their mother's house, he accepted an invitation to spend the night. Before sunrise, the bedraggled beggar had the two men handcuffed and making the long walk back to the camp he and his posse had set up.

Burton uses Reeves's penchant for disguise as evidence that he might have been the model for the Lone Ranger—that and the fact that many of the fugitives he arrested ended up in the Detroit House of Corrections, in the same city where radio station WXYZ introduced the masked lawman on January 30, 1933. It's a stretch, I'm thinking, but there's no doubt that Reeves deserves a more prominent place in popular culture, including a show of his own.

He's about to get a couple. The man from Cranfills Gap, Taylor Sheridan, the actor/writer/producer/director behind *Yellowstone* and other gargantuan hits, will soon begin shooting the *Yellowstone* spinoff *1883: The Bass Reeves Story*. David Oyelowo, the British actor who played the Rev. Martin Luther King Jr. in *Selma*, will star as Reeves in the six-part limited series, with Houston native Dennis Quaid as U.S. marshal Sherrill Lynn.

Burton, who discovered Reeves when he was a youngster yearning to find a Black Wyatt Earp, told me that actor and director Morgan Freeman also has a Bass Reeves series in development for Amazon called *Twin Territories*. He's a consultant on the project.

"Black Bass," as he was known, died in 1910 at age seventy-two. Where he's buried, no one knows, Burton said.

THE BLACK SEMINOLE TRADITION
IN THE SOUTHWEST

COMSTOCK

When we're in Marathon, my four-legged pal Buddy (Holley) looks forward to morning runs at Post Park south of town. (Ducks on the pond and gopher dens in the picnic area make for an exciting morning.) Driving down to the park one morning, I glanced, as usual, toward a nondescript hill off to the left, where a chain-link enclosure around a grave site near the top looks out of place among the rocks and brush.

This time I gave in to impulse. Pulling off the road and leaving Buddy in the car, I slithered like a rattler under the bottom strand of barbed wire and trudged through thorny bushes and prickly pear to the top of the rock-strewn hill. Catching my breath—and hoping landowner Susan Combs didn't have a remote camera pointed in my direction—I surveyed the timeless view a fellow named Blas Payne had so often appreciated during his long life: striated rocks in shades of ocher angling upward like a ship's prow, rugged hills fading into blue-gray mountains, miles and miles of empty brush-covered ranching country. The enclosure where I stood protected two gravestones: Catarina B. Payne, 1904–1996, and Blas M. Payne, 1901–1990.

Information about Catarina Payne is hard to come by, but her husband is a Big Bend legend. A cowboy, a horse handler, and for years a foreman on the Combs Ranch, Blas Payne was heir to a grand tradition in the Southwest, one that needs to be better known. He was a Black Seminole.

The Black Seminole story stretches back to the early 1700s, when the jungle wilderness and malaria-ridden swamps of Spanish Florida became a refuge for runaway slaves from rice plantations in southern Georgia and South Carolina. They found protection by settling near the Seminoles, a confederation of tribes driven south by inexorable European settlement. Intermingling with the Indians, they became known as Black Seminoles.

For more than a century they lived in independent communities with their own leaders. They owned property, carried arms for self-defense, and were often military allies with their Seminole neighbors. All was well until Gen. Andrew Jackson invaded their semitropical fastness.

In 1818 the future president led an American army into Florida to claim it for the United States. The Seminoles, Indian and Black, fought fiercely, but after two wars and a full-scale guerrilla insurrection that lasted years, the might of the American military prevailed. In 1842 the army forced the Black Seminoles and their Indian allies on a punishing trek to Indian Territory (now Oklahoma).

In Oklahoma, the federal government placed them under the authority of the slaveholding Creek tribe. They also were at the mercy of white slave traders. In 1850 a group of Black Seminoles and Seminole Indians fed up with their plight escaped south across dangerous slaveholding Texas and into Mexico, where slavery had been outlawed years earlier. The Mexican government gave them a land grant near Musquiz, a village southwest of Eagle Pass / Piedras Negras, in exchange for protecting the Coahuila–Texas border against Apache and Comanche raids.

As in Florida, their settlement became a haven for runaway American enslaved people. That irritated the Texas Rangers. In 1855 a heavily armed Ranger band splashed across the Rio Grande intent on routing the Seminoles. The Blacks and Indians drove them back into Texas. Many of the Indian Seminoles eventually returned to Oklahoma, but the Black Seminoles remained in Mexico, often forced to fight to protect their community from Comanche and Apache raiders.

After the Civil War the American military desperately needed experienced Indian scouts, translators, and trackers. In 1870 the U.S. Cavalry enticed some of the Black Seminoles—Mexicans called them los Mascogos—to return and join the army, promising them cavalry pay, rations, horses, and land for farming. At least 150 of them showed up for duty at Fort Duncan, near Eagle Pass, where they were officially recognized as the "Seminole Negro Indian Scouts."

Moving to Fort Clark near Brackettville, they engaged the Comanches in numerous skirmishes across West Texas and into northern Mexico. That's how Isaac Payne, a Blas Payne forebear, found himself fighting for his life in spring 1875. Payne, a trumpeter, and two other Black Seminole scouts, Sgt. John Ward and Pvt. Pompey Factor, were under the command of a thirty-two-year-old white lieutenant named John L. Bullis, a New York Quaker who had commanded U.S. Colored Troops during the Civil War. The quartet had tracked down a band of forty or so Comanches driving a herd of seventy-five stolen horses toward the Rio Grande. Engaging the band, Bullis ordered his men to spread out among the rocks, hoping to trick the heavily armed Comanches into thinking they were fighting a force larger than four men.

It worked for about forty-five minutes, but when their forty-to-four ruse was discovered, Bullis and his men made a run for it. The scouts leaped astride their horses and galloped away, but Bullis's horse threw him. Ward happened to glance back, where he saw the lieutenant standing alone and apparently uninjured, firing his carbine at the fast-closing, Winchester-armed Comanches. Alerting his comrades, Ward headed back to help Bullis. Payne and Factor joined him, providing cover fire while Ward locked arms with Bullis and swung him up behind.

"We were at last compelled to give way, as they were about to get around us, and cut us off from our horses," Bullis wrote in his report. "I regret to say that I lost mine with saddle and bridle complete, and just saved my hair by jumping on my sergeant's horse back of him."

For their bravery, Payne, Ward, and Factor received the Congressional Medal of Honor. (Another Black Seminole, Pvt. Adam Payne, received the Medal of Honor for gallantry in the 1874 Red River War.)

The skirmish took place near the confluence of the Pecos River and the Rio Grande, in a deep defile known today as Seminole Canyon. The canyon is also home to Seminole Canyon State Park near the village of Comstock. The park's primary mission is to protect spectacular pictographs drawn on canyon walls eons ago.

Fort Clark, home to the Black Seminoles, is sixty miles east of Seminole Canyon. When their unit disbanded in 1914, the Seminole Negro Indian Scouts were promised land at the fort, but the federal government reneged. The Black Seminoles faded into history, although the Seminole Indian Scout Cemetery Association, based in Brackettville, has worked tirelessly through the years to keep their story alive. The four Medal of Honor winners are interred in the Seminole Indian Scout Cemetery south of Brackettville.

Today their descendants live in Brackettville, Del Rio, Eagle Pass, and other West Texas communities, as well as across the river in Musquiz and elsewhere. Blas Payne spent his whole life around Marathon, working for seventy years on the Combs family ranch. When I wrote about him a few years ago, I interviewed Susan Combs, then the state comptroller, who had known him since she was a little girl.

"He was super good with horses, super good with cattle," she told me. She and her husband named their middle son after him.

The late Lonn Taylor, a former Smithsonian Museum historian who lived in Fort Davis, told me about an East Coast scholar who was convinced that Payne was buried on the hilltop near Post Park because the local cemetery wouldn't take a Black man. Taylor knew otherwise. He knew that Payne had asked permission from the Combs family years before he died. He wanted to be buried on the east side of the hill, he told them. He wanted to see the sun come up.

FINDING CONAN'S CREATOR
IN A LITTLE WEST TEXAS TOWN

O n a wall in the back room of the Howard residence on the edge of town, home in the 1920s and '30s to Dr. and Mrs. Isaac Howard and their son, Robert, is a map of the world festooned with dozens of multicolored dots. Each dot represents a visitor to the little white-frame house; a quick glance suggests that more countries are dotted than not.

The visitors are pilgrims, so to speak, journeying to a West Texas hamlet, population 982, to pay homage to a young man whose stories, more than eighty years after his death, continue to be devoured by millions. Like Elvis devotees journeying to Graceland, they are drawn to the home (now museum) of a small-town Texan who arguably invented the "sword and sorcery" genre of fire-breathing dragons, beautiful princesses, evil wizards, and indestructible warriors.

Robert E. Howard is his name. In the words of East Texas novelist Joe Lansdale, the man from Cross Plains "is a writer of worth, working with dirty hands and a snotty nose sometimes, but flexing strong muscles that even hardcore literature fanatics ought to take note of."

In a career lasting barely a dozen years, Howard published more than two hundred fantasy stories in *Weird Tales, Action Stories, Oriental Stories, Argosy, Spicy Adventure, Strange Detective,* and other pulp magazines of the day. He also published some 350 poems and three novels.

His best-known character is, of course, Conan the Barbarian, denizen of the Hyborian Age, a world that in his creator's fevered, fertile mind existed after the destruction of Atlantis and before the rise of known ancient civilizations. Before *Game of Thrones* and similar fantasies, Howard invented epochs, created races, and wrote with such charged energy that his work, as Stephen King has noted, "nearly gives off sparks."

When I dropped by the Howard house one morning, museum volunteer Arlene Stephenson was showing four visitors the site of a recent National Park Service archaeological dig near the back door. Three of the visitors were from Atlanta, and their friend was from Green Bay, Wisconsin. They were football fans flying into Dallas to take in the NFL draft, but they had rented a car and had made the four-hundred-mile round trip to this town near Brownwood to visit the home of "the single-most energetic, page-turning writer I've ever known."

That's how Chris Wiese described Howard as he and his friends stood in the backyard near the dig, where archaeologists a couple of days earlier had uncovered a cellar containing canned preserves. Weiss told me he discovered the king of pulp fiction as a young-ster. Thus inspired, he now runs Holistic Designs, an Atlanta-based multimedia company that produces online games set in pre-ancient civilizations like the Hyborian Age. For Wiese and his wife, Tracy, only the Green Bay Packers approach the star-crossed writer from Cross Plains as objects of their affection.

Robert Ervin Howard was born in 1906 in Peaster, west of Fort Worth. His father was a country doctor who moved his family every year or so from one oil-boom town to the next until 1919, when he set up his practice in Cross Plains. Howard's mother, Hester Jane Ervin Howard, suffered from tuberculosis and was preternaturally devoted to her only child. The intense feeling was mutual, perhaps in part because the doctor was emotionally distant from his son and couldn't fathom his burning desire to be a writer.

In one of a number of letters to H. P. Lovecraft, master of the classic horror tale, Howard said he wrote his first story when he was eight or nine and began trying to get stories published at fifteen. He was eighteen when he made his first professional sale, the short story "Spear and Fang," in which a Cro-Magnon rescues his mate from a Neanderthal. *Weird Tales* bought it, the first of many Howard tales the magazine would run.

Banging out stories on an Underwood typewriter in his tiny bedroom, shouting out the slam-bang dialogue to himself as he typed, Howard would be lost in other worlds for as many as eighteen hours at a stretch. In the middle of the Depression, he was supporting himself as a writer by age twenty-two.

"Conan simply grew up in my mind a few years ago," Howard said, "when I was stopping in a little border town on the lower Rio Grande. I did not create him by any conscious process. He simply stalked full-grown out of oblivion and set me at work recording the saga of his adventures."

Howard scholars believe the "little border town" was Mission, where the Howard family visited in 1932. A memory of the Hill Country outside Fredericksburg seems to have given him a terrain for his hero. Apparently the "endless vista—hill on hill, slope beyond slope, each hooded like its brothers" transported Howard out of Texas and into Conan's exotic world.

In his brief career, the prolific Howard also wrote about boxers, gunslingers, bootleggers, Comanches, detectives, Texas Rangers, and pirates. Constantly feeding the maw of the pulp magazines, creating new characters, new worlds, and new adventures, he wrote like a man possessed.

On June 11, 1936, the thirty-year-old writer learned that his mother would probably not regain consciousness from a coma brought on by her TB. He walked out to his car and took a .38 Colt automatic out of the glove compartment. Sitting behind the steering wheel, he held the gun to his right temple and pulled the trigger. He lived for eight hours; his mother died the next day.

For a long time, Cross Plains didn't know what to make of the strange young man who had lived and worked among them. "My mother told me that if you saw him walking down the street, you'd cross to the other side," a Cross Plains native recalled.

His acolytes knew. In 1986, half a century after Howard's death, a gathering of sword and sorcery fans and scholars converged on Cross Plains for a weekend of sharing about their favorite writer. They've made their way back every year since. Arnold Schwarzenegger's *Conan the Barbarian* movies in the early 1980s also contributed to a resurgence of interest in the author, as did the 1996 film *The Whole Wide World*, starring Vincent D'Onofrio as Howard and a young Renée Zellweger as his girlfriend, Novalyne Price Ellis. (The movie is based on Ellis's memoir.)

In 1992 Project Pride, a volunteer group dedicated to preserving local history, purchased the Howard house. Stephenson was part of that effort.

"We were determined to do something to make Cross Plains proud," she told me. "We realized we had a history here, and we should take pride in it."

On the second weekend in June, as usual, Cross Plains welcomes several hundred "Howard Heads" back to town. The locals have come to realize that a little country town struggling to stay alive needs every edge it can find.

"At first," Stephenson said, "their concept of Howard was Conan, a big, muscular guy dragging women around. We had to get people past that. Now they're realizing the world is at our doorstep. People come here. And they spend money."

BARBETTE, THE TEXAS TOAST OF PARIS

ROUND ROCK

I know Round Rock Donuts, the Round Rock Express, and Round Rock's Sam Bass, the Old West bank and train robber who met his ignominious end in a pasture west of town. Until recently, I did not know Barbette, an exotic Texan whose path from Round Rock to Paris and back began atop his mother's backyard clothesline.

Barbette's nephew, Charles Loving, tells me that one reason I'd never heard of his uncle is because Round Rock's city fathers in the early 1990s rejected a proposed statue of their accomplished native son. "Nobody gay ever came from Round Rock!" they said. (That probably wasn't the official response, but that's how Loving remembers it.)

Whether Round Rock has produced any notable gay people is, of course, arguable. What's inarguable, I'm willing to bet, is that this fast-growing Austin suburb—no doubt with a usual assortment of gay, straight, bisexual, and transgendered residents—is the only town in Texas that's produced a cross-dressing tightrope walker who became the toast of Paris in the 1920s and '30s. (And I don't mean Paris, Texas.)

He was born Vander Clyde Broadway in 1899. (Some sources say 1898; some say 1904.) When he was about eight, his mother took him to a circus in Austin, and the youngster responded to the high-wire act with gape-mouthed awe. Forget the lion tamer and the rambunctious clowns, the beautiful girls smiling and waving from atop lumbering elephants; back home in Round Rock, young Vander informed his mother that he was going to run away and join the circus as a wire-walker. She urged him to wait at least until he graduated from high school, which he did—as valedictorian at age fourteen. Meanwhile, he picked cotton in the summer to earn circus-going money.

He taught himself to walk the wire by practicing for hours every day and learning to balance atop his mother's backyard clothesline. Loving says he also got to where he would walk across the big iron bridge over nearby Brushy Creek—walk across atop the bridge, that is.

His big break came shortly after high school when he noticed a billboard ad for an aerialist to work with the Alfaretta Sisters, a circus act from Italy. One of the two sisters had died unexpectedly, and the other was conducting auditions in San Antonio for her replacement. After the young man from Round Rock got the job, his new partner—who, incidentally, was the wife of a blackface comedian named Happy Doc Holland, the Destroyer of Gloom—asked if he minded dressing as a girl. "I didn't, and that's how it began," he recalled.

Developing his solo act for the vaudeville circuit, he took the name Barbette because it sounded French. He made his solo debut at the Harlem Opera House in 1919, performing trapeze and wire stunts high above the stage in a sumptuous ball gown, blond wig, and ostrich-feather hat.

"I'd always read a lot of Shakespeare," he told Francis Steegmuller in a 1969 profile in the *New Yorker*, "and thinking that those marvelous heroines of his were played by men and boys made me feel that I could turn my specialty into something unique. I wanted an act that would be a thing of beauty—of course, it would have to be a strange beauty."

"He was definitely androgynous, both an athlete and a beautiful woman," says Bill Lengfelder, a professor at Southern Methodist University who teaches movement to actors. "That psychological flip is what fascinated me. Deep down inside, he really was both."

Lengfelder, the author of a play about Barbette, had another thought: "I believe Vander Clyde Broadway / Barbette understood humanity as only someone who could balance true nature. I think Caitlyn Jenner is a publicity seeker and not the same as the Round Rock, Texas, champion of androgyny."

Barbette made his European debut in 1923 when the William Morris Agency sent him first to London and then to Paris. At the Casino de Paris, the Moulin Rouge, the Empire, the Medrano Circus, the Alhambra Theater, and the Folies Bergère, he was the talk of American café society and the Parisian avant-garde.

His admirers included Picasso, Diaghilev, and the photographer Man Ray. He also toured Europe and America with Ringling Bros. and Barnum & Bailey Circus. He told Steegmuller he traveled "with twenty-eight trunks, a maid, and a maid to help the maid."

Jean Cocteau, the French poet, novelist, and dramatist, fell in love with him. "The young American who does this wire and trapeze act is a great actor, an angel, and he has become the friend to all of us," he wrote a friend. "Go and see him, be nice to him, as he deserves, and tell everybody that he is no mere acrobat in women's clothes, nor just a graceful daredevil, but one of the most beautiful things in the theatre."

In 1926 Cocteau wrote an essay about the nature of art in which he observed that Barbette "transforms effortlessly back and forth between man and woman." The young performer's femaleness, he wrote, is like a cloud of dust he throws into the eyes of the audience to blind it to the masculinity he needs to perform his acrobatics. "That blindness is so complete," he noted, "that at the end of his act, Barbette does not simply remove his wig but instead plays the part of a man. He rolls his shoulders, stretches his hands, swells his muscles. And after the fifteenth or so curtain call, he gives a mischievous wink, shifts from foot to foot, mimes a bit of an apology, and does a shuffling little street-urchin dance—all of it to erase the fabulous, dying-swan impression left by the act."

Barbette's nephew says that a Russian sailor in the audience one night became so distraught when he realized the enticing woman on the wire was actually a man that he drew a pistol and shot himself. A few nights later Barbette, still distraught himself over the incident, fell. His injuries, combined with a bout of pneumonia, ended his career.

He came back to Texas in 1938, lived with a sister in Round Rock and Austin, and for more than thirty years worked as a choreographic consultant on Broadway shows and Hollywood movies, including *Some Like It Hot* and *The Big Circus*. About Austin, the continental sophisticate told Steegmuller, "I have to say that, apart from my family, everything offends me."

He lived with chronic pain from illness and the long-ago injury. "He asked me for the poison, an overdose of Quaaludes," Loving told me. (He affects a French accent.) "Charles, can you get these for me?" he said. "I thought about it, but then I thought, 'I know what he's going to do!'"

Loving refused, but his uncle Vander was undeterred. On August 5, 1973, he died of a drug overdose. His ashes are buried in Round Rock Cemetery on Sam Bass Road.

Feuding and Fighting,
Mayhem and Madness

One objection I have heard voiced to works of this kind—
dealing with Texas—is the amount of gore spilled across the pages.
It cannot be otherwise. In order to write a realistic and true history
of any part of the Southwest, one must narrate such things,
even at the risk of monotony.

— ROBERT E. HOWARD,
letter to August Derleth, March 1933

THE TEXAS PIG WAR

AUSTIN

I n the middle of the night out in Marathon recently, Buddy the
dog started barking with an urgency befitting a bloodhound on
the trail of Bonnie and Clyde. Jolted out of sleep and stumbling
into the living room, I peered through the glass front door and saw
the objects of his agitation: a half-dozen javelinas trotting across
the porch, pausing to munch on prickly pear growing between the
porch and the street. Watching the porcine procession in the dark
of night, I suddenly imagined myself Jean Peter Isidore Alphonse
Dubois, the self-styled Comte de Saligny.

Saligny, the chargé d'affaires of the Kingdom of France to the
fledgling Republic of Texas, never saw a javelina, as far as I know,
but he did have to deal with its cousin, *sus scrofa domesticus*, the
domesticated hog. Hungry porkers belonging to an Austin hotelier
made his life miserable. They ravaged his garden and broke into his
house, where they wallowed among his fancy French bedclothes.
They possibly changed the course of Texas history.

Staring at the tusked troupe on the Marathon porch the other
night, I shuddered at the thought of a rip-snorting javelina home
invasion. Quickly opening the front door, I threw a tangerine at
the sturdy-looking leader of the pack. The mushy missile was all
I could find on the spur of the moment, unlike Saligny, who had

his butler shoot a few grunting miscreants, thus igniting the fabled Texas Pig War.

To appreciate the significance of the Pig War, it's best to keep in mind this description of Saligny, in the words of historian Nancy N. Barker, writing in a 1969 issue of the *Southwestern Historical Quarterly*: "The little French dandy with his cellar of fine burgundy wines, his stable of blooded horses, his irascible temperament and unabashed lobbying has been the butt of a thousand jokes." The finicky Frenchman found himself in the crude new settlement called Austin because France had recognized Texas as a sovereign nation and negotiated a trade agreement that covered import duties on Texas cotton tied to those imposed on French silks and wines. The shaky new Republic desperately needed money, $5 million or so, perhaps in the form of a loan from France.

To cement relations with its potential benefactor, the Texas Congress in 1841 took up the Franco-Texian Commercial and Colonization Bill, which would have allowed eight thousand French immigrants to settle on three million acres of land. The bill also stipulated that the French military would build and maintain a string of twenty forts between the Rio Grande and the Red River, where ten thousand troops would be housed tax-free for twenty years. A corporation would run the operation, with Saligny himself playing the role of a French Stephen F. Austin.

In *Seat of Empire: The Embattled Birth of Austin, Texas*, Jeffrey Stuart Kerr quotes a French newspaper editor: "Texas will become, so to speak, an independent French colony, appertaining to herself alone and costing us nothing."

The bill passed the Texas House but died in the Senate when acting president David Burnet let it be known he would veto it.

For Saligny, who desperately wanted the bill to pass, the pigs were merely an added humiliation. When the Frenchman first showed up in Austin, he lived in the city's only hotel, the Bullock House on the northwest corner of Congress and Pecan (now Sixth Street). The owner, a rough-and-ready frontiersman from Tennessee named Richard Bullock, had little use for the cultivated Frenchman. Saligny, who despite his airs was a faux count, firmly believed he deserved much better than the Bullock House (or Austin, for that matter), so he persuaded his government to purchase twenty-one acres just east of town.

Commissioning the design and construction of an elegant home on a hill with commanding views of the wooden shanties, rude cabins, and muddy streets that comprised the capital city, he moved into a "wretched wood shanty" on Pecan Street near the Bullock House until the French legation was completed. That's where the pigs found him.

Bullock let his pigs run loose. In early Houston, free-range pigs acted as unofficial trash collectors; maybe his pigs performed the same function for Austin. Saligny did not appreciate their utility, particularly when they started bashing down the wooden fence around his kitchen garden, trampling the vegetables he had planted, and eating the corn he had stored for his horses. And then—*quelle horreur!*—they got inside the house. Showing a discriminating taste rare among Texas hogs, they lounged on his bed, chewed up silk sheets and pillowcases, and topped off their French meal with a dessert of diplomatic papers.

Austinites, who had taken to calling Saligny "No-Count," showed no sympathy, so the Frenchman took matters into his own hands. He ordered his butler, Eugene Pluyette, to shoot the pigs on sight, which he did on February 11, 1841, felling between five and twenty-five of the intrusive porkers. When Bullock sought damages for the loss of his pigs, Saligny invoked diplomatic immunity and the "Law of Nations" in response. Bullock responded by chasing down the unfortunate servant Pluyette, pelting him with rocks, and then beating him with a stick before a rowdy crowd on an Austin street.

On February 18, 1841, the French government lodged an official protest, and Texas secretary of state J. S. Mayfield called a judicial hearing three days later. Saligny refused to appear before a Texas court and also ordered Pluyette not to appear. Although the innkeeper was indicted for beating the butler, his bail was promptly paid by treasury secretary John Gordon Chalmers, who had undiplomatically opined that Bullock should have shot the little Frenchman.

On April 5, 1841, Saligny fled Austin for New Orleans, never to return. The loan Texas desperately needed fell through as well, along with the Franco-Texian legislation. Barker says that the Texas Republic's flirtation with the French was probably doomed to fail anyway, but she and most historians agree that pigs in the bedroom didn't help. Texas turned to her American cousins for assistance, and the rest is American history, not French.

Saligny, who ended up back in France, never lived in the ambassadorial residence he commissioned, but the French legation still exists, situated on a hill a couple of blocks east of I-35, at Ninth and San Marcos Streets. The beautiful wood-frame house and grounds reopened recently after being closed for a couple of years for extensive renovations.

THE BATTLE OF MEDINA

LEMING

San Antonio is famous worldwide for its Mexican heritage, but the city's connection to Mother Spain sometimes gets overlooked. Even Texans, I suspect, sometimes forget that one of the state's oldest cities was founded by Spaniards in 1718 and that Texas itself was part of Spain for more than 130 years.

With San Antonio's tricentennial celebration in full swing, the spotlight for the next several weeks will be on Spain, with a spectacular exhibition of paintings by Spanish artists at the San Antonio Museum of Art, an "Ole, San Antonio" celebration in the Pearl District, and other Spain-related events.

"Spain is such a fundamental part of what San Antonio is, and that is being recognized and celebrated this summer," historian and urban designer Sherry Kafka Wagner told the *New York Times*.

Thanks to my old friend Sherry's observation, I found myself standing in a field of grass and weeds off Highway 281 about twenty miles south of the city in search of another notable Spanish connection. In the morning stillness of the countryside, I tried to imagine the clang of swords, the roar of cannons, and the screams of dying men who fought and killed one another in the field before me on a hot August day in 1813.

It's called the Battle of Medina, and the history books have always given it short shrift, even though, with more than a thousand casualties, it's the bloodiest battle ever fought on Texas soil. The engagement remains obscure despite the fact that it prepared the way for Anglo-American settlement in the coming decade. We're not even sure exactly where it happened.

Armies may have clashed in that field off 281; a small monument erected by an amateur historian marks the spot. Or they may have met a few miles away, in what's now rolling pastureland on the Toudouze Ranch off San Antonio's Loop 1604. Old belt buckles, cooking items, and musket balls have been found buried in the soft sandy soil. Except for cows seeking shade under groves of oak and mesquite a couple of days ago, the land looked like it could have been a battle site.

Or the armies fought near the current intersection of two gravel roads in northern Atascosa County, near the Leming community. That's where the state historical marker says it may have taken place. The marker stands at the corner of an empty lot where barrel racers practice. Despite periodic pronouncements from historians and archaeologists, no one has ever fixed the exact site, perhaps because it was a running battle and artifacts may be buried over a wide area.

Here's what we do know: At a time when Mexico and Latin America were in revolt against Spain and the United States was at war with England, Mexican revolutionary José Bernardo Gutiérrez de Lara and U.S. army Lt. Augustus Magee, with assistance from the United States, organized an expedition to capture Texas. The self-proclaimed Republican Army of the North, flying an emerald flag, crossed from Louisiana into Texas on August 7, 1812, and soon captured Nacogdoches and several small East Texas settlements before continuing westward.

In San Antonio on April 6, 1813, the rebels proclaimed independence for the State of Texas under the Republic of Mexico. Their green banner would fly over Texas for about four months.

On August 4, Gen. José Álvarez de Toledo y DuBois, a Cuban-born revolutionary, deposed Gutiérrez. (Magee had died earlier in the year.) That same month, Gen. José Joaquín de Arredondo y Mioño organized a Spanish royalist army of some 1,830 men and marched them from Laredo toward San Antonio to put down the insurrection. Toledo had an army of about 1,400 men composed of Anglos, Tejanos, Native Americans, and former royalists. Hoping to spare San Antonio the ravages of war, the Tejanos in Toledo's army persuaded him to meet the enemy south of town.

On the night of August 17, as historian Robert H. Thonhoff tells the story in the *Handbook of Texas*, Toledo set up camp about six miles from Arredondo's camp between the Atascosa and Medina Rivers. Toledo's plan was to ambush the royalists as they marched into a defile along the Laredo road.

The plan fell apart the next morning. Trudging through deep sandy soil in dense woods, the republicans suddenly found themselves within firing range of the royalists, who had set up breastworks on high ground. On a hot summer day, the two armies fought from about noon until 4 p.m. in a furious battle involving infantry, cavalry, and artillery. The republicans broke ranks and ran, and the battle became a slaughter, with some 1,300 men either killed or later executed. The Spanish lost fifty-five men.

The crushing defeat put an end to the rebellion, and San Antonio endured martial law. Arredondo had the wives, daughters, and other female relatives of the rebels imprisoned, where they were raped, brutalized, and forced to convert twenty-four bushels of corn a day into tortillas for the occupying army. Their children begged in the streets for food. For a month after the battle, Arredondo executed ten men a day in the Plaza de Armas, now the site of city hall, and placed their heads on spikes.

The Spanish forces, by the way, included a nineteen-year-old lieutenant who would find his way back to the San Antonio area some years later. In his official report, Arredondo mentioned "Don Antonio Santa Anna" as one of three men who "conducted themselves with great bravery" in the 1813 battle. It's been said that the man who would later proclaim himself "the Napoleon of the West," the general who laid siege to a mission called the Alamo in 1836, learned his tactics on and off the battlefield from Arredondo.

DANGER STILL LURKS IN SALT FLATS

SALT FLAT

"Don't even think of trying to drive out on those salt flats," Shirley Richardson told me one afternoon as we stood outside the Salt Flat Cafe and bus stop. Shirley's grandparents opened the café in 1929 in what's now a desolate ghost town near the base of the spectacular Guadalupe Mountains. She had to close it eight months ago, she told me, after she fell and broke her knee, wrist, ribs, and shoulder chasing after a dog that had run out on the highway with a butane truck bearing down.

The salt flats cover a portion of her family's ranch, five miles east of the café in Hudspeth County in West Texas. They're a remnant of an ancient shallow lake from the Pleistocene Epoch, approximately 1.8 million years ago. From U.S. Highway 62, the surface looks densely packed, like the Bonneville Salt Flats in Utah. It's not.

We talked a bit about the café and about how the little town has hosted a couple of flight pioneers. Amelia Earhart touched down in Salt Flat three times in the 1930s, Shirley said. Amazon founder and CEO Jeff Bezos had the café's green chili enchiladas not long ago. The vast acreage across the road from the café is part of his Blue Origin spaceflight services company.

Driving past the flats again, I noticed a westbound car slow and pull off the pavement. I glanced over my shoulder and saw the driver do exactly what Shirley had warned about. The car plowed through the glistening gray flats for about fifty yards before bogging down, tires spinning as the driver got out and tried to push. I made a U-turn and stopped on the shoulder. A young man in shorts and a T-shirt, arms waving, came running through the salty muck toward my car.

The salt flats have caused consternation before. They even sparked a short-lived war.

To get a sense of their significance, imagine a train of sixteen cottonwood carts pulled by sixty yokes of oxen making its creaking, tedious way across the arid waste of far West Texas. The eighty or so men driving the stolid animals are *salineros*, salt gatherers from the El Paso Valley communities of Ysleta, Socorro, and San Elizario. Salineros have been making the 160-mile trip since the 1700s.

Nearly all of the residents downriver from El Paso, most of them farmers and livestock grazers, were Mexican in language, ethnicity, and culture (and still are). Salt was integral to their daily lives. Not only did they rely on it to preserve meat and cure hides; they also sold it to silver miners around Chihuahua, who used tons in the refining process. And they sold to the U.S. army.

Under Spanish law, the salt beds were common property. After the Mexican War, they became unclaimed lands under American law, available to anyone who filed on them. The Mexicans—who became Mexican Americans when the Rio Grande changed channels in the 1820s—believed that everybody had a right to the salt, a right guaranteed by the Spanish crown centuries earlier and affirmed by the Treaty of Guadalupe Hidalgo. Enduring the heat and the threat of Apache attack as they had for generations, they never thought to file claims.

They didn't realize that after the Civil War and the chaos of Reconstruction, their world was changing drastically. The late Paul Cool, author of the definitive history of the Salt War, *Salt Warriors:*

Insurgency on the Rio Grande, put it this way: "If salt was the excuse for war, the underlying reason was this struggle between the rights of the community and those of hustling individualists."

The hustlers included El Paso businessmen W. W. Mills, Albert J. Fountain, and Louis Cardis, who attempted to acquire title to the salt deposits and charge for the resource. Fountain was elected to the Texas Senate expecting to secure title for the people of the El Paso area. When Mills and Fountain began feuding, Cardis and Mills joined forces with Charles H. Howard, a Missouri lawyer and former Confederate officer. Cardis helped get Howard elected district attorney, but then Howard turned on Cardis.

In September 1877 Howard arrested two San Elizario residents heading for the salt beds. An angry mob captured and held the district attorney for three days at San Elizario. He gained his freedom by vowing to give up claim to the salt beds and leave the state. He retreated to nearby Mesilla, New Mexico, but soon returned and killed Cardis in an El Paso store. Arraigned for the murder, he was placed under bond to appear in court in March.

The mule-headed Missourian couldn't leave well enough alone. In December a wagon train of Mexicans from both sides of the border left the valley, headed for the salt deposits; Howard filed suit. When he went down to San Elizario to press charges, he and a handful of Texas Rangers were besieged by a mob of several hundred locals. Howard and the Rangers took cover in the Rangers' fort, and a gun battle raged for four days. On the fifth day Howard gave himself up. The Rangers also surrendered, believing they had an agreement with the insurgents to free Howard.

That's not what happened. On December 17 he was lined up against a wall before a firing squad of eight men from Mexico. Cool quotes an eyewitness account: "When all was ready, Howard spoke.

He could not speak Spanish very fluently, but enough to make himself understood; he said, 'You are now about to execute three hundred men,' then, baring his breast, he gave the word, 'Fire!'"

They did. The insurgents executed two of Howard's associates as well but allowed the Rangers to leave the fort after forfeiting their arms. Within a few days, several detachments of troops and a posse of American citizens had arrived in San Elizario, where they killed or wounded an untold number of residents. Most of the insurgents had already fled into Mexico, and no one was ever arrested or brought to trial. President Rutherford B. Hayes and Army Gen. Philip Sheridan resisted public pressure to invade Mexico.

There were no salineros from San Elizario in Salt Flat when I visited, but there was one very distressed young man from Japan. "Toku" (he asked that I not use his full name), his wife, and his eight-year-old son, Japanese citizens living in New Jersey, were on the last day of their American Southwest vacation when they got stuck on the flats. I drove Toku back to Shirley's place, where she greeted him with, "You stupid idiot!"

Despite his limited English, Toku understood what she had said. "Yes, idiot, yes," he said. Shirley told him it would cost five thousand dollars to get a tow truck from El Paso, eighty-seven miles away. His mouth fell open.

Despite her exasperation, rescuing people from their temporary folly on the flats is a common occurrence for Shirley. She led us into the café where she started making calls to tow-truck operators in Van Horn. No one could help. She mentioned to Toku that the Greyhound to El Paso would be coming through in about half an hour. Passengers have to stand beside the road and wave it down.

As Toku considered the bus option, his cell phone beeped. It was his wife back at the car. A man driving a pickup had stopped and was able to pull the car out.

The young man from Japan, the dried muck on his shins and shoes a souvenir of his West Texas adventure, was near tears. "Such wonderful people," he said, smiling at Shirley and me. "Such wonderful people."

AN EARLY SERIAL KILLER'S
ETERNAL MOONLIGHT

AUSTIN

For Austinites of a historic bent, news that local police and the FBI relied on radio towers tracking cell phone usage to pinpoint the location of Austin's recent serial bomber brought back memories. They recalled another set of towers and the story of another serial killer—America's first—who terrorized the city long ago.

Austin's "moonlight towers" have been a part of the urban fabric for so long that they're essentially invisible, although you've seen a movie version of one if you're a fan of Austin filmmaker Richard Linklater. You'll remember the "moon tower" from *Dazed and Confused*, the 1993 stoner classic set in Austin on the last day of school in 1976. In the movie, little of note happens throughout the day until Wooderson—played by Matthew ("all right, all right, all right") McConaughey—gathers his buddies together for a nostalgic nighttime keg party at the foot of one of the venerable light towers.

Veteran *Texas Monthly* writer Skip Hollandsworth makes the connection between the towers dispensing perpetual moonlight and the serial killer who terrorized the city for more than a year, beginning in late 1884 (long before the term "serial killer" was coined). In his award-winning book *The Midnight Assassin*,

Hollandsworth describes Austinites living in fear—"on edge," to reprise an oft-used term—as a diabolical killer used axes, knives, an ice pick, and long steel rods to rip apart young women while they slept in their beds. Seven women and one man fell victim to the murderous spree.

Early victims were African American maids and housekeepers, often living in servants' quarters or "alley houses" in the backyards of the city's wealthiest white families. Some victims were only injured; they were able to make their escape or scream in time to scare off their attacker. None could identify him. Others weren't so fortunate. In December 1884 an African American cook named Mollie Smith was found sprawled in the snow next to the outhouse behind her employer's home, a gaping hole in her head. She was the first.

The early incidents were dismissed as "negro murders" until Christmas Eve 1885, when a white woman named Sue Hancock, described by a reporter as "one of the most refined ladies in Austin," was discovered by her husband in their backyard, close to where the Four Seasons Hotel is today. Her head had been split open by an axe; a sharp, thin object was lodged in her brain. About an hour later, another prominent white woman, Eula Phillips, was found dead in the wealthiest neighborhood in the city, near the old, now-empty Austin Public Library on Guadalupe Street. These two killings, as Hollandsworth tells the story, "brought Austin to the brink of chaos."

Austin city fathers first saw the moonlight towers at the World's Industrial and Cotton Centennial Exposition, a kind of world's fair held in New Orleans in spring 1885, a few months after the two white women were murdered. At night the exposition grounds were bright as day, thanks to 125-foot-high towers that held giant, newly invented "arc lights," each light emitting "36,000 candlepower."

"The Austin visitors were impressed," Hollandsworth writes, "but for many of them, the lamps appeared to be more like a pointless curiosity than a helpful invention. Why, they asked, would anyone want to go to such expense to light up a city throughout the night? What possible purpose would it serve?"

Those questions were easier to answer a few years later when a newly constructed Colorado River dam and an adjoining power station provided enough low-cost electricity to run electric streetcars and install as many streetlights as the city wanted. Instead of electric streetlights atop twenty-foot-high poles, the choice for almost every other American city, the mayor and city aldermen decided to go with the arc lights atop very tall towers.

The Fort Wayne Electric Company fabricated thirty-one wrought-iron and cast-iron towers, each 165 feet tall and weighing approximately five thousand pounds. They were shipped in pieces to Austin and erected in 1894–95. Tall and stately, supported by slender guy wires, they reminded admirers in decades to come of miniature Eiffel Towers.

Unlike other cities, where the lamps illuminated shopping districts or railroad depots, Austin positioned them all over town so they would cover as much ground as possible. Chicken owners were concerned their hens wouldn't know when to stop laying eggs in "the city of eternal moonlight," but the birds turned out to be smarter than that. Even tower opponents had to admit that the lights would make it harder for a person up to no good to hide in alleys or shady lots along hilly residential streets.

When the lights were switched on for a test on May 5, 1895, "there was a sudden blinding flash and the town was in a blaze of white light that hid the rays of the moonlight," an *Austin Daily Statesman* reporter observed. "In every nook and corner the brilliant lights sent their shooting rays and the whole face of creation was transcendent."

In more than a decade of research, Hollandsworth never found any official statements that directly connected the arc lamps to the murders. The *Daily Statesman* reporter seemed to be alluding to something, though, when he wrote that Austin's residents had spent years "groping around in that darkness that threatened the life and safety of all." Hollandsworth believes the allusion is telling.

Fifteen moonlight towers still stand. Although the pale glow of their lamps is barely noticeable among the much brighter electric and mercury lights closer to the streets, they're not going anywhere. In 1976 they received a National Historic Landmark designation. Hollandsworth notes that the city's application for landmark status described the towers "as quaint, nostalgic relics of a time gone by, as much a part of Austin as the streetcars are of San Francisco."

And the killer, the sadistic midnight assassin? Who knows? Despite several arrests and three trials, no one was ever convicted. His identity is a mystery to this day. Some say he ended up in London. Some say he was Jack the Ripper.

THE YOUNG MAN IN THE BIG BEND
WHO CAME TO NO GOOD END

ALPINE

Visitors to Big Bend National Park might or might not know Townsend Point as one of the sentinels towering over the Chisos Mountains basin. Even though it's 7,500 feet high and is named for the man considered the father of the park, the travel guides and hiking trail booklets don't always mention it.

The same with E. E. Townsend, whose colorful, eventful life could fill a year's worth of columns. A West Texas cowboy, a Texas Ranger in the 1890s, a federal border agent, a Brewster County sheriff, and a state representative, Townsend dealt with smugglers and Mexican border bandits; got shot in the chest and survived, thanks to a bullet-deflecting notebook in his vest pocket; and, as a lawmaker, pushed for years to save Big Bend for the public's enjoyment. His decades-long crusade culminated in fall 1943 when Big Bend State Park passed into the national park system.

From a thick and tattered scrapbook that his wife, Alice, kept over the years—now in the Bryan Museum in Galveston—and from Townsend material in the Big Bend archives at Sul Ross State University, I was able to piece together the following curious tale from Townsend's tenure as sheriff during the early 1920s.

Then as now, the vast ranch country around Alpine can be eerily quiet, particularly at night. Under a glittering array of stars, you might hear the yip of coyotes or the screech of a scavenging owl; for sure you'll hear, every four or five hours, night and day, the mournful keen of a freight train's whistle.

On the night of January 24, 1922, a long westbound freight pulled into town, and a brakeman heard something else, something that sounded like groans coming from an empty boxcar. He slid open the door, thrust his lantern inside, and was shocked to see a semiconscious man lying on the floor with a handkerchief tied over his mouth as a gag.

The brakeman called for help and then summoned the sheriff. When Townsend and his deputies arrived from their office a few blocks away, they were able to get the young man out of the boxcar and onto a cot inside a nearby work train. An examination showed that he had been shot in the back and struck repeatedly on the head with some kind of instrument, later determined to be a pistol.

Near death, he managed to tell Townsend that his name was Clifford H. Rogers, that he was from Austin, and that his father was a conductor on the Houston and Texas Central Railroad.

An army veteran and carpenter by trade, Rogers, twenty-seven, had been in Philadelphia where, on January 1, according to the *Alpine Avalanche*, he had married "a beautiful young lady" and was on his way to California to take a job; his new wife planned to follow. "Just why he was traveling by the box car could not be developed," the newspaper reported.

Rogers was able to tell authorities that his assailant was his boxcar traveling companion. Mrs. Clay Roberts, a café owner in nearby Marathon, confirmed that two young men had eaten supper at her place the night before, that Rogers had paid for both of them with a twenty-dollar bill, and that she had watched them hop the westbound freight.

"It is hell to feed a man and then have him shoot you in the back for twenty dollars," Rogers told authorities. He died the next day.

Later that morning Townsend's deputy, T. I. Morgan, arrested a young man in the small town of Toronto, six miles west of Alpine. His name, he said, was Harvey Leon Hughes; he was twenty-one, from Delphos, Ohio; and he was traveling cross-country to Los Angeles when he happened to meet up with Rogers. Hughes had on his person Rogers's money, watch, fountain pen, and other personal effects. He told Townsend that he and Rogers had quarreled between Marathon and Alpine and that Rogers had insulted his mother.

Less than a month later a Brewster County jury rejected Hughes's claim of self-defense, despite what the *Avalanche* described as "one of the most brilliant pleas ever heard in a Brewster County court" by defense attorney Walter Haynes.

"Unmoved," the newspaper reported, "as if not realizing what the verdict means, the boy showed no emotion and paid little attention to the awful words that placed the hangman's noose around his neck."

In late October, Townsend and Morgan were in San Antonio to attend court proceedings, and Morgan's wife was left in charge of the jail. Checking on her young prisoner at about eight in the evening, she discovered that Hughes had somehow picked the lock to his cell and was hiding in the corridor. She struggled with him, but he ran out into the cold, rainy night.

"The sheriff's department and the county attorney have made free use of the wires and a net has been spread for Hughes which, sooner or later, will entangle him in its meshes," the *Avalanche* predicted.

It was sooner. Three days later he was discovered, cold and wet, hiding in a cave near Toronto, within sight of Alpine.

As Hughes's date with destiny approached in spring 1923, the Texas Legislature was considering a bill that would change the state's method of execution from hanging to electrocution. In the Townsend scrapbook is a copy of a typed letter Townsend sent to Gov. Pat Neff requesting that the young man's execution be postponed, so that he could die in the electric chair.

Townsend emphasized that he wasn't asking for mercy, just a postponement. The governor refused. He also refused a petition from a group of Alpine citizens asking that he commute Hughes's sentence to life in prison.

Despite his violent crime and his brief escape, the petition suggests that Alpine residents had come to feel a certain pity for the "unfortunate young man." In an autobiographical essay published in the *Avalanche*—"my first writing on any subject"—Hughes described a youth in and out of reform schools, where he "became acquainted with the different types of criminals, which had a great deal to do with my future."

On a Saturday morning in April the condemned man was escorted up the steps of gallows erected the day before on the north side of the courthouse. Accompanying him were a minister, Townsend, and other officials. As Hughes stood listening to the minister's prayer, a hemp-rope noose around his neck, he received what historian Mike Cox calls "a final courtesy from Sheriff Townsend." To spare him from knowing the exact moment of his death, the sheriff sprang the trap before the minister intoned amen.

Hughes was the only man ever legally hanged in Brewster County and one of the last hanged in Texas. (The last was in Brazoria County on August 31, 1923.) The next year, the state began using Ol' Sparky, considered more humane than hanging.

OL' RACEHOSS SURVIVED BURNING HELL

He was Albert growing up on the wrong side of the tracks in Longview during the Depression, but once Albert Race Sample made it to "Burnin' Hell"—the inmates' name for the notorious Retrieve Prison Farm near Angleton—he became Ol' Racehoss. Prison guards bestowed that name in grudging recognition of his cotton-picking prowess. From dawn until past dusk, summer after summer, the guards on horseback, shotguns at the ready, watched him surge through endless rows in vast fields, picking bolls under a burning sun with the quick hands of the slickest crap-shooter in East Texas. No one else on the prison farm could keep up with the wiry, light-skinned Black man.

As a young man, Ol' Racehoss was in and out of Retrieve and other Texas prisons for more than seventeen years. Once he got out—and stayed out—he wrote a book about his experiences. Published in 1984 and recently reissued, *Racehoss: Big Emma's Boy* is one of the most affecting memoirs I've ever read. The late Studs Terkel got it right when he called it "an outcast's eloquent testament to life."

Life was cheap where Sample grew up. His father, a white man, was a prominent Longview cotton broker who acknowledged his son but wouldn't take him in. (This was deep East Texas in the 1930s, of course.) His mother, the formidable Big Emma, was a professional gambler, a bootlegger, and a prostitute, "busy tricking seven days a week." Although she physically abused her little boy when she drank, he was her "houseman," beginning at age four.

"I sat on the case of bootlegged whiskey bottled in half-pints until somebody wanted one," Sample recalled. "I collected the money and gave each customer a dipperful of water with which to wash it down, if it was bought by the shot. Between sales, I kept a sharp lookout for the police and a keen eye on the dice when they rolled off the blanket so nobody could switch in some crooked ones. When Emma was shooting, I watched the cigar box she kept her loose change in so nobody would 'clip' her."

He was on his own by six, hopping freights and roaming the country by twelve, and serving a twenty-year sentence for armed robbery by the time he was twenty-two (to be served concurrently with the thirty-year sentence he had received for robbery by assault).

His fellow inmates in the segregated facility were the most incorrigible Black convicts in the Texas prison system. He quickly learned it was called Burning Hell for a reason.

The Retrieve Unit, now known as the Wayne Scott Unit, had been a plantation. A South Carolinian named Abner Jackson got it going in 1839 and, according to the *Handbook of Texas*, constructed a two-story mansion, slave quarters, a sugar house, and ovens. Around 1842 Jackson sold half of his interest to James Hamilton, former governor of South Carolina and an emissary to Europe for the Republic of Texas. By 1860 the Retrieve slaves were producing more sugar than almost any plantation in the state, and its owners were the second-largest slaveholders in Texas.

In the early 1900s the plantation, lacking the labor of enslaved people, leased convicts from the state to work the cotton, corn, and sugarcane fields. The state bought the 7,424-acre plantation in 1918 for $320,829.60 and continued to use the property as a prison farm into the 1990s, its seven hundred hardworking inmates making it one of the most productive in the state.

Life in Burnin' Hell during the 1950s and '60s would have been familiar to the enslaved people who worked the land more than a century earlier. Sample and his fellow inmates, some four hundred in all, ran the daily risk of being worked to death or shot to death by sadistic, racist prison guards, most of them ignorant and uneducated. Both the guards and their prison system bosses would have sneered at any thought of rehabilitation.

Sample's description of the brutality, insanity, and grinding racism of prison life in the mid-twentieth century is as powerful as anything I've read in years. He had an ear for dialogue, particularly African American dialect, and the stories he tells—sad and enraging, to be sure, but just as often funny—are unforgettable.

"It's an unbelievable story," David Dow, a professor at the University of Houston Law Center, told me. "I don't think I got out of my chair until I finished it."

Dow, founder of the Texas Innocence Project, wrote the foreword to the new edition. "I think the story is still a very contemporary story," he said. "He's writing about an era that's superficially very different, but there's still racism. It's of a different nature."

Sample survived, thanks in large part to a mysterious spiritual moment he experienced during a brutal twenty-eight-day stint in solitary. Released from prison in 1972 at age forty-two, he became the first ex-con in Texas to serve as a probation officer. He received a full pardon and restoration of all civil rights in 1976. In 1982 Sample and his wife, Carol—they met in Houston in 1975 and married the next year—quit their jobs, sold their car, and moved into a rent house in Dripping Springs. Sample, who had worked for a couple of years at the *Forward Times* newspaper in Houston, sat down at a typewriter and began writing his book, with Carol editing at her own typewriter across the room. It took them nine months.

"He just sat down and cranked it out," Carol Sample told me as we sat in her kitchen in far East Austin. "It was something he had to do." And now there's something she has to do. Her beloved Race died of cancer in 2005, leaving her with thirty years of funny, poignant, incredible stories still to tell. She finished her sequel to *Racehoss* a couple of months ago.

I promised not to tell too many of the stories she shared with me, but one I can't resist. Young Albert, she said, taught himself to tap-dance by watching Bojangles teach Shirley Temple in movies he saw at Longview's Rembert Theater (admission nine pennies). Soon he was tap-dancing for spare change on downtown streets, and not long afterward he made his way to Dallas where he danced two shows nightly at a nightclub. He made five dollars a show, although the aunt he was staying with usually stole it while he slept.

One night the little boy met his idol, the former wife of the club owner, Jack Pepper. The beautiful, blonde-haired young woman asked him to dance with her, and after rehearsing for about an hour they performed a number together. Ginger Rogers called him Lil' Bubba.

THE SORROW AND STRENGTH
OF SUTHERLAND SPRINGS

SUTHERLAND SPRINGS

On a sunny Sunday after church, I'm walking behind a young man rolling himself in his wheelchair along a newly built wooden ramp. He comes to a ridge in the boards and hesitates; I reach for the handgrips to give him a slight push.

"Whoa!" he exclaims. "I wasn't ready for that."

During the past six months of his life, thirty-four-year-old Kris Workman, married and the father of a little girl, has had to get used to a lot of things he wasn't ready for. On a Sunday morning in November 2017, he was one of about fifty worshippers at the First Baptist Church of Sutherland Springs when a gunman stormed into the sanctuary and started spraying bullets from an AR-15. Twenty-six people died that morning, including children and three generations of one family. Workman, shot in the back as he huddled under a pew, was left paralyzed from the waist down. Absent the miracle his mother fervently expects, this former college tennis player will be in a wheelchair for the rest of his life.

"I don't have nightmares; I don't have PTSD symptoms," he told me. "I guess the one regret I have is not being able to run and play with my daughter."

The crush of media that overwhelmed this town east of San Antonio has gone away. The huge satellite trucks have lumbered on to the next disaster. Gaggles of intrusive print reporters juggling notebooks and tape recorders, broadcast reporters wielding microphones and cameras, are no longer accosting people after church or outside the Valero station across the highway or at their front doors.

A few reporters have lingered, seeking to capture, if you will, the rest of the story. We want to know how this community copes long term with suffering in the wake of outrage, disaster, and tragedy (whatever the word should be). We want to know whether good can emerge from such a deep well of pain. Is there anything a little town and a country church can teach the rest of us?

As one of those reporters who returns periodically to this quiet, unassuming community—and who tries not to be too intrusive with his questions—I've come to realize one thing: when fickle public attention eventually gets distracted, when the White House and the National Rifle Association and good-hearted donors from around the world move on, residents and church members won't be. When they wake up in the morning, when they go to bed at night, they live with "the incident" (the generic term they've come to use for the deadliest mass shooting at a place of worship in American history). Like residents of West, the Central Texas town that experienced a deadly fertilizer plant explosion five years ago, or like Gulf Coast Texans in the wake of Harvey, moving on, literally or figuratively, is not that simple.

I think of Workman, of course, who was able to return to his job with a San Antonio–based computing company only a couple of weeks ago. (He's also the church worship leader.) I think of his mother, Julie Workman, who was under that pew with her son and survived. Both insist that their faith will see them through.

I think also of David Colbath, a lay minister at the church who has worked in construction for most of his life. Colbath, forty-six, was sitting in the pew nearest the shooter when he burst in and started firing. Bullets riddled his arm and hand and burrowed into his chest and buttocks. A bullet remains lodged in his side near his heart. He's still undergoing physical therapy and will be for months. He's also undergoing therapy of a different sort as he copes with the memories of a morning "when bullets were flying all over" and the nightmares that visit him at night. Encouraging his fellow survivors not to be reluctant to get help, he tells them about the therapist at Brooke Army Medical Center who counsels veterans of Afghanistan and Iraq.

"Warriors have sat in that same chair you're sitting in," the therapist told Colbath. "They've seen much violence. They're the toughest men in America, and they were bawling." Colbath's message is that there's no shame in seeking help.

I think also of Oscar and Alice Garcia, longtime Sutherland Springs residents who weren't members of the church at the time of the shooting but who know everybody in town. Alice was born and raised in Sutherland Springs and remembers playing basketball in the quiet streets as a kid and attending vacation Bible school at the church, even though she and her family were Catholic. "People still hung their clothes on clotheslines," she recalls.

On that Sunday they were leaving their church in nearby La Vernia when they began to get frantic texts about a shooting in Sutherland Springs. Arriving back home a few minutes later, they ran to the church, saw with horror what had happened, and then, desperately looking for some way to help, opened the door of the community center. The old building a couple of blocks from the church became the heart of the community every day for the next couple of weeks.

Usually a place for birthday parties, family reunions, and annual festivals, the center was an impromptu meeting spot for families affected by the shooting and then a place for receiving donations, food, and flowers. First responders and anyone else in the community came by for meals at all hours of the day.

The Garcias, both in their forties, would stay until midnight and be back the next morning at seven. Oscar, who delivers septic tanks for a company in nearby Floresville, juggled his job and his duties at the center.

"We were looking for a ministry, and we became the ministers," he told me. They switched their memberships to the church nearby that needed so much in those first few weeks.

"I believed in God," Alice said, "but I can say my love for God has grown significantly. I found out what my purpose in life was. To serve others."

More than a century ago, Sutherland Springs was a place of healing. In the early 1900s people rode trains out from San Antonio to bathe in and drink the mineral waters of nearby Cibolo Creek. Alice and Oscar Garcia would like to think that in the wake of unspeakable tragedy, their town will again be a place of healing—for townspeople and the church and for others far beyond Sutherland Springs. From both the community's sorrow and its strength, they pray that good can emerge.

Postscript: Thanks to funds from the Southern Baptist Convention and donations from around the world, members of the First Baptist Church of Sutherland Springs were able to build a majestic new church building adjacent to the small chapel where the shooting occurred. Members decided to leave the chapel intact as a memorial. Kris Workman, David Colbath, and other survivors still face challenges coping with their injuries, mental and physical, even as they've gotten on with their lives. My book about the shooting and its aftermath, *Sutherland Springs: God, Guns, and Hope in a Texas Town*, was published in 2020.

Remarkable Texas Women

The single truly essential ingredient
that every Texas woman must possess is this:
She must know she is exactly as special
as the state she comes from.

— SARAH BIRD,
A Love Letter to Texas Women

THE REMARKABLE ANA MARÍA CALVILLO

WILSON COUNTY

On a June morning in, let's say, 1815, you're riding west toward San Antonio de Bexar along El Camino del Cíbolo when a dust cloud signals an approaching rider. As the distance between the two of you closes, you make out a majestic white horse and, astride the horse, a handsome woman, her long black hair fluttering like pennants from beneath her wide-brimmed hat.

You recognize the rider as the remarkable Doña Ana María del Carmen Calvillo, descendant of early San Antonio settlers, former wife of anti-Spanish rebel Juan Gavino de la Trinidad Delgado, and, since her father's violent death the year before, flamboyant owner of Rancho de las Cabras along the west bank of the San Antonio River.

Rancho de las Cabras, or Goat Ranch, was established in 1731 by the Franciscan friars of Mission San Francisco de la Espada, known today as Mission Espada, the southernmost of the five missions clustered near the San Antonio River. According to a 1745 report, the mission maintained large herds of cattle, sheep, goats, horses, and oxen, but early settlers complained that the animals were trampling their crops. The friars dispatched Native American vaqueros, probably teenagers, to herd the animals thirty miles downriver to the Goat Ranch.

These early-day cowboys lived at the lonely outpost, where they were vulnerable to attacks by Lipan Apaches, Comanches, and other raiders. At least once a week, they likely herded sufficient cattle and goats back to town to supply mission residents with beef and cabrito.

According to the Texas Beyond History website, a 1772 inventory of Mission Espada reported that the ranch consisted of four jacales, structures of upright poles with thatched roofs, one of which was sometimes used as a church or shrine; corrals and pens; and a fenced field for corn. A later account mentioned that the ranch was home to twenty-six people, including herders and perhaps their families.

"It's the only known extant mission ranch that still has standing architecture," National Park Service archaeologist Susan Snow told me.

The mission operated the ranch until secularization in 1794, when the Spanish government sold church properties to private owners. The rancho's new owner was Ignacio Francisco Xavier Calvillo, an early San Antonio settler. When he was killed by bandits in 1814, his daughter took over the ranch.

By all accounts, Ana María del Carmen Calvillo was a remarkable woman. Born in San Antonio in 1765 to Calvillo and his wife, Antonia de Arocha, a descendant of Canary Islanders, she was the eldest of six children. She married Juan Gavino de la Trinidad Delgado around 1781. The couple had two sons, both of whom died young, and three other adopted children.

Between 1811 and 1814 Gavino was part of an active and often bloody rebellion around San Antonio against the Spanish crown. María left her husband during this period, perhaps to protect the family's land holdings, and let it be known that he was dead. He wasn't.

"She could be something of a scoundrel," said Tambria Read, a Floresville High School art teacher and knowledgeable local historian. "For several years, Doña Ana María del Carmen Calvillo was my research passion."

On April 15, 1814, her father, Ignacio Calvillo, was murdered during a raid initially thought to have been perpetrated by Indians. A later investigation revealed that the attackers included Calvillo's own grandson, disguised as an Indian.

With both father and husband no longer in the picture, Ana María Calvillo gained control of Rancho de las Cabras. Unlike their American counterparts, women in Spain and Spanish Texas had the right to hold property under their own names and could sell any property they had owned before marrying. Property purchased or inherited during the marriage belonged to both spouses.

On August 28, 1828, Ana María Calvillo formally petitioned the Mexican government for a new title to the ranch. It was granted the next month. In the coming years, she increased her livestock operation to perhaps two thousand head of cattle, added an irrigation system and a mill, and expanded her crop production. She also managed to get along with nomadic Indigenous tribes by offering them cattle and a camping site when they passed through the area. She died in 1856 at age ninety-one and bequeathed the ranch to two of her adopted children.

Archaeologist Snow said that artifacts suggest the ranch "changed in use through time," perhaps evolving into a central gathering place for the area or an informal inn for travelers.

In 1976 the Texas Parks and Wildlife Department acquired ninety-nine acres from private owners, including what remained of the old ranch structures. Without funds to preserve the crumbling rock walls of the compound, the department buried the ruins in sand to prevent further erosion and vandalism. In 1995 the National Park Service acquired the property, which is now part of the World Heritage Site of the San Antonio Missions National Historical Park.

National Park Service biologist Greg Mitchell oversees the site, just off Highway 97 five miles south of Floresville. The dirt road to the ranch is unmarked at the highway and is normally closed to visitors, although archaeologists from the University of Texas at San Antonio and the National Park Service have excavated the site. Area Girl Scouts and the Junior Historians Club from Floresville High School, under Read's sponsorship, have helped clear trails. Maybe by the fall [2018], Mitchell said, the site will be open to the public, perhaps two weekends a month. He'd love to find additional volunteers to help him maintain it.

On a recent hot, steamy morning, we ambled along a quarter-mile hiking trail through rangeland Mitchell hopes will revert to native prairie. Jumbled sandstone rocks, once part of ranch fortifications, jutted up through their protective covering of sand and grass. We walked past a depression in the ground that would have been a stone quarry and descended a steep ravine into lush, thickly forested San Antonio River bottomlands. Mitchell said alligators have been known to lurk in a nearby oxbow.

I told Mitchell I had read that Ana María's ghost—astride a white horse, her long hair flying—had appeared off and on through the years. Since the Michigan native is often alone at the site, I wondered if he had seen her. He said he had not.

Knowing her, of course, is more important than seeing her. As Read has written, "Doña Ana María del Carmen Calvillo was a strong, courageous, and spirited Spanish/Texas woman, experienced in riding horseback, handling guns, managing her ranch, and getting along with others, and a proud steward of her land."

This almost forgotten woman, an integral part of the state's ranching heritage, deserves to ride her white horse into the history books.

STEPHEN F. AUSTIN'S FAVORITE COUSIN, MARY AUSTIN HOLLEY

ANGLETON

Growing up on the family farm in Central Texas, my dad detested his given name. He hated "Horace" so much that most people who weren't family knew to call him Holley. Where his folks got the name, nobody knew, and I suppose now we never will. (He could have used his middle name, but "Moten" was hardly an improvement.)

The name became all the more intriguing when I discovered that Stephen F. Austin's favorite cousin, Mary Austin Holley, was the widow of one Horace Holley, a Yale-educated Unitarian minister and president of Transylvania University in Lexington, Kentucky. Horace Holley was sailing from New Orleans to Europe in 1827 when he died of yellow fever and was buried at sea off the Dry Tortugas in the Gulf of Mexico.

It's unlikely that a farm couple in Texas in the early years of the last century would have named a son after a New England–born minister and educator who had lived and died decades earlier. As best I can tell, there's no family connection. Maybe my grandparents—Charlie and Mary Della—had studied Latin, or maybe they just liked the alliteration.

Whatever the connection—or nonconnection—I've long been interested in Horace Holley's widow, in part because of Mary

Austin Holley's ties to her famous cousin but also because her book, *Texas: Observations, Historical, Geographical, and Descriptive, in a Series of Letters,* is the first known English-language history of Texas. That book, based on her 1831 visit to her cousin's colony, was published in 1833. Three years later an expanded version, titled simply *Texas,* became a bestseller and an influential immigrants' guide for Americans "bound, like myself, to the land of promise."

"She was an excellent pianist and spoke French, German, and Spanish and was most agreeable in conversation," a contemporaneous friend recalled. That's the impression I got from her biography, published years ago. She was refined, sophisticated, and well educated. But Mary Austin Holley, I rediscovered recently, was much more than a cultured lady, as a cursory reading of her diary and letters reveals. (Her papers are housed at the Dolph Briscoe Center for American History at the University of Texas.) She was a graceful and perceptive writer, to be sure, but she also was witty, engaging, and adventurous. She knew politics and business and was well traveled. In line after line of elegant handwriting, "this very superior woman," as Austin described her, comes wonderfully alive.

In a diary entry for April 31, 1835, she's aboard the schooner *San Felipe* on a five-day voyage from New Orleans to the mouth of the Brazos. She and her fellow passengers, sixty in all, are deathly seasick. "I lay on my berth or sat listlessly on the deck—too inert from the recent commotion of my stomach to make further application of my better powers," she writes.

As they approach their destination, the sea and her stomach settle, and she dares to be risqué: "For the luxury and novelty of the thing, there being no gentlemen about, I went without stockings and with the thinnest covering in other respects."

She recounts the latest gossip from Brazoria: Mr. Stephenson has killed Mr. Berryman in a duel, muskets at ten paces.

"Mr. B," she writes, "was the lover of Mrs. Stephenson, now parted from her husband in consequence & went to N Orleans last trip of the San Felipe. On the dead body was found a lock of the lady's hair, perforated by that ball that reached his heart. On the envelope was written, as on a bundle of her letters. To be placed in my coffin. Were they so disposed of? No: the injured husband wrote to the faithless wife that the hair she had placed on her lover's bosom, proving no shield, was bathed in his blood."

She offers a parting thought: "Women—when bad—how bad!!"

Her pencil sketches of Houston, the capital city newly hacked out of a pine forest, are the earliest pictorial documentation of the first capitol building and homes of prominent residents. The town makes a good appearance, she writes, but "is not healthy—several bilious cases exist at present—contains 1800 to 2000 inhabitants—80 sailors are now in Houston. The houses generally are of one story—a few have 2. Two large hotels with galleries above and below." In long, chatty letters to her grown children, amid talk about politics and land deals and clothes she's making for the grandkids, she imparts the latest gossip: "The old Gen. Gaines is married to a widow of 25 with 3 male children. He is in his dotage and though lost to . . . is no great gain. How unlucky all our beaux get married—or die—or something!!!!!!"

When Holley arrived in Texas in 1831, she hadn't seen her famous cousin for twenty-five years, and, as historian H. W. Brands points out, "she might not have seen him for twenty-five more had her husband not suddenly died, leaving her to puzzle out how to support herself and her young son." She decided that writing about Texas might be a profitable endeavor.

Brands surmises that Austin as a young man had a crush on his cousin, who was nine years older. Her visit to Texas rekindled those feelings.

"Mrs. H. is a divine woman," Austin told James F. Perry, his brother-in-law. He hoped to persuade her to relocate permanently to Texas.

Jennifer Parsley, a Brazoria County historian with a special interest in early Texas women, believes the cousins intended to marry. She suggests that Austin saw her in Lexington, her home, on an 1835 trip to raise funds for the Texas cause. "He either proposed or seriously thought about it," Parsley says, basing her theory on letters the two wrote each other.

However close the couple became during their brief reacquaintance, she was "his sounding board and confidant during a very crucial period, from 1831 to 1832," Parsley says.

Holley never lived in Texas. Her beloved cousin, his body worn out from his exertions on behalf of Texas and his two-year imprisonment in Mexico City, died in 1836 at age forty-three.

In an 1844 letter she told Austin's sister, Emily Austin Perry, that she was planning to write "a memoir of our lamented Stephen," intending to "bring out his name from the rubbish that surrounds it, in bright relief before the Country and the world."

Her sister-in-law discouraged her: "For you know that their [sic] were many persons whose names would appear that took a very decided part in those trying times to defeat Stephen in all his endeavors and plans for the prosperity of his adopted country, some are dead and many of them are still living, and those that are dead, have relatives who would be mortified to see their names brought before the publick at this time."

Perry advised Holley to "lay it by to be published in after years." The book was never written. Mary Austin Holley died of yellow fever in 1846, nineteen years after the same disease took her husband, Horace.

THE THORNY ROSE OF TEXAS

KNICKERBOCKER

On a quiet afternoon in Memphis, Tennessee, as I imagine the scene, a woman stands ironing in the living room of her modest red-brick home. The year is, say, 1950. Neighbors for whom she sews and takes in laundry have no idea that her quiet life is about as distant from her previous life as Memphis is from Wyoming. They could not imagine that the Cowboy State is where she and a gang of West Texas outlaws robbed trains, or that she rode with a couple of desperadoes called Butch Cassidy and the Sundance Kid.

She was born Laura Bullion in 1876 and came with her mother and two siblings to this community near San Angelo to live with her mother's parents, the Bylers, after her father disappeared. The settlement along spring-fed Dove Creek, where Serena and Elliott Byler built a house and raised vegetables, was not far from a ranch where four New Yorkers were trying to make a go of it raising sheep. The New Yorkers named their ranch headquarters after Washington Irving's fictional character, Diedrich Knickerbocker.

By the 1880s the town that had grown up around the ranch boasted two saloons, three stores, a combination blacksmith-undertaker's business, and two hotels. Less than a quarter-mile southeast was Rock Village, a Mexican community of sixty rock houses as well as a Catholic church, a wool house, and a blacksmith shop.

The Bylers were a churchgoing family, doing their best to raise Laura and her brother and sister, even when the children's mother, Fereby, stayed gone for weeks at a time with a succession of boyfriends. In addition to their grandchildren, the Bylers raised sweet potatoes, including a five-and-a-half-pound giant, the *San Angelo Standard Times* reported in summer 1886. Five years later the newspaper reported that Laura had made the sixth-grade honor roll with a ninety-nine average. Her mother had died a year earlier.

Laura wasn't content with raising potatoes, sweet or otherwise. At fifteen, she headed for the big city, San Antonio. Seeking steadier work than she could find in Knickerbocker, the petite, dark-haired teenager took the name Della Rose and was soon one of the favorites at Fannie Porter's Sporting House, a popular brothel on the southwest corner of Durango and San Saba Streets. (Butch Cassidy may or may not have made his famous bicycle ride on the street out front.)

Laura stayed in touch with folks back home, including a gang of young cowboys who had determined that cattle rustling was more lucrative than cattle raising. Tom "Black Jack" Ketchum and his brother Sam, Ben "Tall Texan" Kilpatrick, Will "News" Carver, and Dave Atkins soon graduated from rustling to robbing stagecoaches, banks, and trains. They ranged across West Texas and the Panhandle into New Mexico Territory and points north. By 1895 these wayward sons of Knickerbocker had a girl riding with them.

Laura—aka Della Rose—didn't just hold the reins of getaway horses while Black Jack and the boys dynamited the railcar or relieved passengers of their money and valuables. She could ride and shoot as well as they could. Dressed as a man, she was likely to be the masked bandit muttering "Stick 'em up" at terrified passengers. She also fenced stolen goods.

Barbara Barton, a retired public schoolteacher and longtime Knickerbocker resident, has written several local histories, including one about the Knickerbocker Six, *Den of Outlaws*. "What was it?" I asked her by phone. "Maybe something in the water?"

Barton laughed. "They all came from families that really tried to do the right thing," she said. "They just decided the outlaw life was a better way of making a living."

And make a living they did, for a few years. In her book, Barton describes a Union Pacific train robbery near Tipton, Wyoming, in 1900. The Texans rode off with $55,000 in their saddlebags.

Wyoming, of course, was Butch Cassidy country. The Knickerbocker gang not only rode with Cassidy and his Wild Bunch but also hid out with them behind the Hole in the Wall, the hidden gap in a red sandstone escarpment in Johnson County, Wyoming. Legend has it that the Wild Bunch nicknamed Laura the Thorny Rose during a winter's stay at the hideout. That's also where she met Etta Place, the beautiful woman who traded her life as a schoolteacher to be with Harry Longabaugh, alias the Sundance Kid.

With local lawmen and Pinkerton detectives hot on their trail, the Knickerbocker outlaws one by one met their demise. Black Jack Ketchum was among the first. He got shot up during an attempted train robbery in Union County, New Mexico, in 1899. Arrested and confined to prison in the New Mexico State Penitentiary in Santa Fe, he swallowed pins trying to commit suicide and had his bullet-mangled arm amputated by prison doctors. New Mexico hanged him in 1901.

Laura Bullion's lawless years came to an end that same year. Planning to spend their share of a $110,000 take from a Great Northern Railway robbery in Montana, she and Ben Kilpatrick traveled to Saint Louis, where they checked into the Laclede Hotel as Mr. and Mrs. J. D. Rose. The couple spent some of the banknotes they had stolen in a jewelry store, and the notes ended up in a Saint Louis bank. The Pinkerton detectives pounced. When they arrested Laura, they found $8,500 in banknotes in her valise.

In a November 13, 1901, story complete with hand-drawn illustrations, the *Houston Daily Post* reported that Kilpatrick—the authorities initially identified him as Harry Longabaugh (the Sundance Kid)—would be charged with forging signatures on banknotes and having in his possession stolen banknotes. A Great Northern fireman came to Saint Louis and recounted how Kilpatrick clambered over the coal tender and into the locomotive, where he brandished two revolvers.

The *Post* story doesn't mention Laura, although the drawing shows her with short hair and wearing a man's suit and hat.

She spent nearly four years behind bars in Jefferson City, Missouri; Kilpatrick spent a decade in the federal penitentiary in Atlanta. When she got out, she moved to Atlanta to be near him and, according to Barton, bought an interest in a boardinghouse. Not allowed to visit her friend, she wrote a letter, noting that she intended "to live and make an honest living and live down as much of the past as possible." Not yet thirty, she kept her word for the next five decades.

Kilpatrick went back to robbing trains after he was released until he was shot through the eye by a Wells Fargo agent near the far West Texas town of Dryden in 1912. Laura spent time in Texas and Birmingham, Alabama, before settling in Memphis in 1924.

A woman stands ironing. Did she wonder, on long afternoons, staring down at a blouse on the board before her, making sure the hem was straight, how she came to be the girl she once was? Maybe the loss of her mother at an early age affected her more than anyone could know. Maybe she just hated sweet potatoes. She died on December 2, 1961, at age eighty-five.

The little town Laura fled began its decline long ago—"with the advent of the automobile and improved road systems," says the historical marker across the road from the venerable community center. Today it's a San Angelo bedroom community of ranchettes and comfortable ranch-style homes. Nothing is left of Rock Village.

Knickerbocker doesn't commemorate Laura Bullion and her train-robbing pals. In *Den of Outlaws*, Barton includes a picture of her tombstone in a Memphis cemetery. The inscription reads:

Freda Bullion Lincoln
Laura Bullion
The Thorny Rose
1876–1961

GUNSHOT VICTIMS KNEW TO CALL DR. SOFIE

BRAZORIA

This coastal-bend town between two rivers calls itself "the cradle of Texas," with good reason. Jane Long, Stephen F. Austin, Sam Houston, James Fannin, Mirabeau B. Lamar, Dr. Anson Jones, and William Barret Travis all spent time in the area during the early decades of the nineteenth century. If you were a "war dog" or a "crazeorian," as agitators for Texas independence were labeled, chances are you did your plotting in Brazoria.

I was poking around Brazoria County a few days ago, looking for information about Mary Austin Holley, Austin's favorite cousin, when I came across an early Brazorian barely known beyond the county, even though she certainly deserves to be. I found her—found a life-size mannequin of her, that is—at the Brazoria County Historical Museum.

Dr. Sofie Herzog practiced medicine in Brazoria from the 1890s into the early years of the twentieth century. A general practitioner and the first woman to serve as head surgeon for a major American railroad, she wore a necklace of twenty-four bullets she had extracted from Brazoria-area gunshot victims. The necklace was her good luck charm, she said.

Her bullet-extracting technique was unique. Instead of probing the wound with a finger, potentially causing further injury and infection, she positioned the victim in such a way that gravity "would bring the bullet to her" within twenty-four hours. For an abdominal wound, for example, she would suspend her patient a couple of inches above the bed. She reported to a medical conference that every one of her first seventeen patients was up and about by the twelfth day, "ready to shoot or be shot at any time."

This fascinating woman was born Sofia Deligath, the daughter of a physician, in Vienna, Austria, in 1846. At age fourteen she married another prominent Vienna physician, Dr. Moritz Herzog, and the couple had fifteen children, including three sets of twins. Eight died in infancy.

In 1886 Moritz Herzog accepted a position at the U.S. Naval Hospital in New York City, and his wife, between the many births and deaths, somehow found time to study medicine in New York. She returned to Vienna for further study and earned a medical degree from the University of Graz. She practiced medicine for nine years in Hoboken, New Jersey. Her husband died in about 1895.

The Herzogs' youngest daughter, Elfriede Marie, met a Brazoria merchant named Randolph Prell, who was visiting relatives in Philadelphia, where she was teaching school. The two were married in Hoboken in 1894. Sofie Herzog decided to join them in Brazoria where, at forty-nine, she resumed her medical practice. Three years after coming to Texas, she became the first female member of the South Texas Medical Association, and in 1903 she was elected vice president of the organization.

"She was a character, almost a caricature," says Dortha Pekar, a local historian and retired Brazoria librarian. Pekar has researched Herzog's life for more than thirty years and keeps her memory alive by impersonating the good doctor for school groups, civic organizations, and Texas history enthusiasts. Pekar says she knows Dr. Sofie so well that her presentations are stream-of-consciousness monologues.

It took a while for locals to grow accustomed to the newcomer. They weren't used to women doctors, particularly women doctors who cut their hair short, wore a mannish, wide-brimmed hat, and favored a tailor-made split skirt when she made house calls astride a horse. One of three physicians in town, she eventually became known, affectionately, as "Dr. Sofie."

She saw patients from all walks of life, regardless of skin color. "She wasn't just a good doctor; she was a good person," a 106-year-old Black man who had known her told Pekar some years back.

With railroads knitting the state together in the early 1900s, Dr. Sofie began treating workers laying track in South Texas for the Saint Louis, Brownsville, and Mexico Railway. Their work was hard and dangerous, and she frequently got called out to repair broken legs, smashed limbs, and other hazards of the trade. Local railroad officials relied on her, and when the position of chief surgeon opened up, they readily endorsed her application. She got the job—until bigwigs in the Saint Louis home office ruled that it was no job for a lady. They insisted she resign.

She refused.

When Pekar channels Herzog, she has her saying: "I was a woman when you hired me, and nothing has changed in that respect since." The officials backed down, and she remained chief railroad surgeon until a few months before her death at age seventy-nine.

During her thirty years in Brazoria, Dr. Herzog operated a drugstore in connection with her medical practice, concocting many of her own medicines. She built a hotel, the Southern, which became Brazoria's social center. She bought and sold real estate. After getting into a dispute with a priest over the neglected Catholic cemetery, she built Brazoria's Episcopal church.

"She had her own way of doing things," Pekar told me, the homemade Herzog mannequin sitting at her desk and perhaps listening in on our conversation.

Her twenty-four bullets, strung between gold links by a Houston jeweler, wasn't her only eccentricity. The drugstore that fronted her office and the office itself became a museum filled with her various collections. She collected walking sticks, carved and painted in many shapes and colors, from around the world. She was an avid hunter, and on the walls were stuffed birds, a javelina head, and antlers.

Animal-hide rugs covered the floors. She skinned, dried, and mounted rattlesnake skins on wide red satin ribbons, and her doctor's kit rested on alligator feet.

She also collected malformed fetuses from miscarriages she attended and kept them in bottles on her office shelves. Her collection, including a newborn with two heads and three arms, went to John Sealy Hospital in Galveston after her death.

In 1913 Herzog married Col. Marion Huntington, a twice-widowed plantation owner. He was seventy, she sixty-seven. They lived on his plantation, Ellersly, seven miles from Brazoria, and she commuted to work each day in her Ford runabout, the first in the area. She also was one of the first Brazorians to own a telephone. Following a paralytic stroke, Dr. Sofie died in a Houston hospital on July 21, 1925. She was laid to rest wearing her bullet necklace.

THE PEARL BREWERY'S SAGA
OF THREE EMMAS

SAN ANTONIO

In the early spring of 2015 the redeveloped Pearl Brewery complex north of downtown opened a boutique hotel in the historic brewhouse, the building with the tower that's been a landmark for more than a century. Managed by Kimpton Hotels, the 146-room inn is called the Emma, in honor of the widow of Pearl Brewery's founder, Otto Koehler.

It was Emma Koehler who managed to keep the Pearl open during Prohibition (1919–33) when almost every other brewery in the state went under. It's an appropriate name in honor of a formidable woman, although it could have been called the Three Emmas. With apologies to the late Paul Harvey, you have to know the rest of the juicy story to understand why.

The Pearl Brewing Company started here in 1883 under a different name and began producing bottles and wooden kegs of Pearl beer in 1886. Otto Koehler took over as president in 1902. Under his leadership, the business thrived, and he and his wife, Emma, built a three-story stone mansion on a hill in the Laurel Heights neighborhood a few blocks west of the brewery.

In about 1910 Emma Koehler was injured in an auto accident, and her husband hired a live-in nurse to see after her. The nurse's name was also Emma. Emma Dumpke, known as "Emmi," was in her late twenties, brunette and petite. Not long after joining the household, she accompanied the Koehler family to Europe on an extended stay.

Sometime later a friend of hers—also a nurse, also named Emma—came by the Koehler home to have coffee. Emma Hedda Burgemeister, in her midthirties, was blonde, gray-eyed, and five feet ten inches tall. Emma Dumpke—let's call her Emma II—told her friend about "the intimate relations" (quoting the *San Antonio Light*) that existed between her and the master of the house.

At some point during the affair, the German-born beer baron and business mogul, one of the richest men in the Southwest, bought Emma II a little house across the river on Hunstock Avenue, just off South Presa. Koehler paid the expenses and gave Emma II $125 a month in spending money. Emma III—the tall blonde—soon moved in as well. Koehler paid her $50 a month and deeded the house to both Emmas. He dropped by once a week or so at night, for two or three hours.

This arrangement lasted until Dumpke (Emma II) informed Koehler that she planned to be married. Shortly before she became Emma Dumpke Daschiel, Koehler proposed to Emma III. She turned him down, she said later, because "Mrs. Koehler was a sick woman, and I would not leave her behind sick and helpless."

On November 12, 1914, at a little after four in the afternoon, Otto Koehler—age fifty-nine and married for twenty-two years—left the brewery in his buggy and drove to the cottage on Hunstock Avenue. The Emmas were both at home. Within a few minutes of walking through the front door, Koehler was dead from bullets to the neck, face, and heart. The shots were fired by one of the Emmas.

According to detailed reporting in the *San Antonio Light*, on that fateful afternoon Koehler brushed past Emma II in the living room and headed straight to the bedroom, where he found Emma III lying on a bed with a cloth covering her eyes. He reportedly tried to kiss her, a quarrel erupted, and Emma III shot him with a .32 revolver.

The Koehler family told the *Light* there had been a dispute over a bill that nurse Burgemeister (Emma III) submitted for Emma Koehler's care. Otto Koehler drove to the house to settle the matter, and when he and Emma III started arguing, she got frightened and went for her gun.

When police arrived at the cottage they found Emma II in the living room with neighbors and Koehler's body sprawled on the living room floor. They also found two pistols and a case knife.

Emma III was sitting on the floor with her head in the lap "of an old man," apparently a neighbor. Her left wrist was bleeding, from what she said was a self-inflicted knife wound. "I'm sorry, but I had to kill him," she told police.

A grand jury no-billed Emma II but charged Emma III with murder. She decided about that time that wounded World War I soldiers needed her nursing skills and decamped to Europe. Surprisingly, she came back to San Antonio three years later to stand trial. Her lawyer was former Texas governor T. M. Campbell.

"It was a sordid story which the unfortunate woman had to tell, but one which held the jury and the courtroom, packed to the utmost with spectators, breathless," the *Light* reported on January 19, 1918. "Miss Burgemeister wore a dress of dark material and a fur hat and muff, her face was covered with a veil."

Emma III told the jury that she killed Koehler in self-defense and to protect the honor of her friend Emma II.

"Did you shoot him on the floor after he was dead?" the district attorney asked her.

"I don't know," she said. "I only know I shot him as he raised the pistol. I thought he would get me again, and I shot him again. Then I raised the pistol to my head and pulled the trigger."

"How many times?"

"I don't know," Emma III said.

"Your aim was better at Mr. Koehler than at yourself," the district attorney wryly observed.

On January 22, 1918, the all-male jury found Emma III not guilty. In 1919 she traveled to New Orleans, where she married a member of the jury. The newlyweds returned to San Antonio to live in the little house on Hunstock.

Emma Koehler stayed in her own house as well. She may have been "sick and helpless" at some point, but, as Elizabeth Fauerso of the Pearl points out, "she was a very strong person, by all accounts. She was very smart and very strategic."

Taking firm control of the company, she kept it going during Prohibition by brewing near beer and operating various businesses. The Pearl got into making ice, bottling soft drinks, advertising, and even auto repair. Koehler, who was just as resourceful during the Depression, retired after almost twenty-six years as head of Texas's largest brewery, but she remained a formidable presence in the company until her death in 1943. The irony, of course, is that she might never have gotten her chance if the two other Emmas had stuck to their nursing.

Fauerso told me that the Pearl is not quite sure how to tell the whole story, although the hotel bar, she said, might feature a new drink. It will be called the "Three Emmas." Its slogan will be "It'll kill ya."

A KING RANCH DAUGHTER RECALLS A TRIPLE CROWN

KINGSVILLE

When Helenita Kleberg Groves turned on the TV in her Alamo Heights home to watch the 2018 Belmont Stakes—with the favorite, Justify, as a potential Triple Crown winner—she remembered another Belmont Stakes, a race she witnessed on a cool and cloudy June afternoon more than seven decades ago.

On that long-ago Saturday in 1946, the nineteen-year-old Vassar College student—then Helenita Kleberg of the King Ranch Klebergs—waited anxiously in her family's box near the finish line. She watched as seven keyed-up Thoroughbreds settled into the starting gate. Along with the rest of the racing world, she would soon know whether Assault, her family's gallant little three-year-old, would become only the seventh Triple Crown winner in Thoroughbred racing history. (Justify would be the thirteenth.)

Groves and others aware of Assault's young life found it hard to believe that he would be on the track, much less vying for a Triple Crown. They knew the horse was lucky to be alive.

A few weeks before the Belmont Stakes, Kleberg had watched Assault overcome eight-to-one odds in a seventeen-horse Kentucky Derby field and defeat the favorite, Lord Boswell, by eight lengths. Soon afterward she watched him defeat the same horse by a neck in the Preakness. Those two victories set the stage for his assault, if you will, on the Triple Crown, a trio of triumphs that guarantees both horse-racing immortality and a whole lot of "smackeroos," as long-ago announcer Bill Stern put it.

"It was incredibly exciting," Groves said in a recent phone conversation. She recalled that at Churchill Downs, she and a Vassar classmate from Louisville named Kitty sat in a box adjacent to a bevy of "tall, attractive young men." They were Yale football players; several became lifelong friends.

At Belmont Park, she recalled, her winning tickets fell out of her raincoat pocket, "and a nice person—I have no idea who he was—saw me drop them and brought them to me." She remembers wearing a dress her mother had made for her.

It was her father, Bob Kleberg Jr.—known as "Mr. Bob"—who got the fabled ranch involved with Thoroughbred racing. In 1934 he brought a horse named Chicaro to stand stud at the ranch, and five years later he paid $40,000 for Bold Venture, winner of the 1936 Kentucky Derby. Bold Venture sired Middleground, winner of the Kentucky Derby and Belmont Stakes in 1950. Bold Venture also sired a short, skinny, chestnut-colored colt that Kleberg's wife, Helen, named Assault.

Most racehorses come from Kentucky, but Kleberg, true to his Texas ranching heritage, had something to prove. "He wanted to raise horses down in South Texas because it would make them tough," said Bob Kinnan, the King Ranch historian and retired manager of the main ranch residence.

As Kinnan explains it, King Ranch has had a proud history from the beginning of breeding quality animals adaptable to the mesquite, huisache, and prickly pear, not to mention the withering summer heat, that are endemic to the South Texas brush country. Whether it's transforming wild mustangs in the 1800s into sturdy, reliable ranch horses or breeding up the cattle herd from tough and rangy longhorns, ranch founder Capt. Richard King and his successors believed the hard land could be an advantage. Why not Thoroughbreds?

Assault's proud heritage—and his South Texas toughness—almost went for naught. As a foal he stepped on a surveyor's spike, splitting his front right hoof. As Kleberg watched the colt limp around the corral, he seriously considered putting him down.

Longtime King Ranch veterinarian J. K. Northway ("little Doc") believed he could repair the hoof, and ranch kineños—Mexican cowboys who had worked on the ranch for generations—thought they could take care of the horse. Juan Silva, a blacksmith on the ranch, forged a therapeutic-type shoe to bind the hoof together, and Lolo Treviño, working with Northway, groomed and cared for Assault as a yearling.

Once Assault started racing—and winning—sportswriters dubbed him the "Club-footed Comet." "He walked crippled, he sprinted crippled, but once he started running, you never saw a limp," Kinnan said. "He was a pretty amazing horse with a lot of heart."

Before a crowd of forty-three thousand at Belmont Park on that June afternoon in 1946, Assault stumbled coming out of the gate but quickly recovered. Taking the lead with two hundred yards to go, he won by three lengths, thus becoming the first horse bred outside Kentucky to win the Triple Crown. He's still the one and only winner from the Lone Star state.

With Fredericksburg native Max Hirsch as his trainer—Hirsch is a legend in his own right—Assault continued racing through age seven. He compiled a record of eighteen wins from starts and earnings of $675,470, making him one of the leading money-winners of his time.

Groves remembers Assault as a favorite of ranch visitors during his long retirement. "He was a good-dispositioned horse," she said. "He wasn't going to bite you or kick you."

Assault died in 1971. The King Ranch hasn't been involved in Thoroughbred racing since the late 1980s, although Groves, who saw her first race at age seven, will tell you that racing is still in her blood. At ninety, she works with her daughter, Helen Alexander, who breeds horses at her Middlebrook Farm near Lexington, Kentucky. The two women have a breeding interest in one of the Belmont entries, Free Drop Billy.

"I did not name him," Groves said, a hint of disdain in her voice. Despite the name, despite his sixteenth-place finish in the Kentucky Derby, and despite thirty-to-one odds at Belmont, Free Drop Billy has a fan in San Antonio. She happens to be a fan who, long ago, cheered on a horse that defied life's odds.

The Particularity of Place

Few people are willing to believe that a piece of the country,
hunted and fished and roamed over,
felt and remembered,
can be company enough.

— JOHN GRAVES,
Goodbye to a River

PANHANDLE TIME WARP
AT THE ALIBATES FLINT QUARRIES

FRITCH

Let's say you're headed northeast out of Amarillo on State Highway 136 toward this unassuming little town on the shores of Lake Meredith. As you get closer to the Canadian River valley just to the west, you notice the terrain beginning to change. The pool table–flat Panhandle gives way to rugged hills and mesas, twisting gullies and draws. The rolling, rumpled-bed look is not what you picture when the Panhandle comes to mind.

Saving Fritch and the Lake Meredith Historical Museum for another day, look for a turnoff on the left about forty miles north of Amarillo; it's easy to miss. The road takes you to one of the most significant prehistoric sites in North America, one I'm guessing many Texans beyond the Panhandle have never heard of. About three miles off the highway is an area Native peoples inhabited for at least twelve thousand years, called the Alibates Flint Quarries National Monument.

On the crisp weekday morning when I showed up at the visitors center, park ranger Joe Mihm told me that Alibates is one of the least visited national monuments in the United States. That meant the stocky white-haired fellow with a ring in his left ear was free, as he usually is, to escort his two visitors—me and a Chicago retiree checking off his national park bucket list—on a two-hour hike into the bluffs and mesas cosseting the center. After a short drive in his pickup, the retired power company lineman from nearby Borger led us up a steep winding trail cut by modern-day Navajo trail builders from Arizona. Hillsides along the trail were rust-red sandstone freckled with white dolomite, a rock similar to limestone.

With a brilliant blue sky as backdrop, the striking red, white, and blue terrain was a pleasant surprise to my Chicago companion, who favorably compared the isolated area to other national parks he had visited. It surprised me too.

We paused occasionally to catch our breath and listen to Mihm's informative minilectures about native plants and peoples. I asked him about the word Alibates, assuming it was some kind of scientific term. I was wrong.

Mihm explained that it was a man's name. In 1877, after the Plains Indians were forcibly removed from the Panhandle, a couple of enterprising Bostonians, W. H. "Deacon" Bates and David T. Beals, established the LX Ranch, which included today's 4,000-acre national monument and the surrounding area. The ranch raised longhorn cattle and eventually grew to more than 187,000 acres, extending from Palo Duro Canyon to the drift fence near present-day Dumas. The LX Ranch was sold in 1884 to the American Pastoral Company of London, along with forty-five thousand cattle and a thousand horses.

In 1906 Oklahoma geologist Charles Gould came to the ranch searching for oil and gas. A local cowboy, Allen "Allie" Bates (presumably Deacon Bates's son), showed Gould around. For some reason Bates was living in a dugout gouged into the side of a ravine, so Gould named the ravine and nearby features after the cowboy, shortening the name to Alibates. The Alibates Flint Quarries

National Monument was established in 1965, the first national monument in Texas.

Our hilltop destination was a group of small quarries where, six or seven hundred years ago, skilled men and women worked flint into tools and weapons revered for their sharpness and efficiency. (Flint is a dense form of quartz.) The quarries are shallow pits littered with rock shards—red, gray, purple, maroon, white, and multicolored—that are the detritus of carefully chiseled spear points, scrapers, drills, awls, knives, and hammers.

"Flint breaks like glass, but it's harder than steel," Mihm said.

Smooth, workable Alibates flint could cut deeply into the flesh of bison and other edible animals and was more durable than similar tools made of bone, wood, or shell. The finished products were so prized that the so-called Antelope Creek People were able to trade them for shells from the Pacific coast, dried fish from the Gulf of Mexico, and animal furs from the Rocky Mountains.

As a gentle hilltop breeze kept things cool, the three of us stared down at a quarry that Native people had worked until sometime before the Spanish explorer Coronado came through the area in 1541. Close to a thousand pits have been found within the monument area.

"The biggest thing was the sharpness and predictability of the stone," Mihm said. "Talking about the greatest scientific discovery, it's not the wheel; it's the sharp edge. For people without metal, it's the sharp edge of survival."

Mihm explained that long before the Antelope Creek People arrived, the Canadian River valley was inhabited by the Clovis culture, paleo-Americans using flint six thousand years before the wheel was invented, seven thousand years before the Egyptians constructed the Great Pyramid, and nine thousand years before the birth of Christ. Following the Clovis people were the Folsom people, who, like the Clovis, were big-game hunters who stalked the giant bison. In the seventh and eighth centuries CE, the Antelope Creek People settled along the bluffs and tributaries of the Canadian, where they built villages of single-story apartments made of dolomite masonry linked together in a contiguous line. (Mihm conducts tours of village ruins every Friday in October.) They left the area in the mid-1400s; archaeologists aren't sure why. Comanches and Apaches arrived soon afterward.

We trooped down from the quarries about noon. My Chicago companion headed west toward Santa Fe and a reunion with his girlfriend, who was celebrating her victory over cancer by running a marathon in Seattle. Not ready to leave the area—an area that felt haunted, as it were, in a good way—I strolled along a winding trail through scrub vegetation not far from the visitors center. My destination was a large rectangular-shaped limestone rock lying flat on the ground near the narrow, red-tinged Canadian. When I found it, I noticed that early-morning dew congealed into ice had partially filled a perfectly rounded cylinder worn into the scarred gray stone. Thanks to Mihm, I knew what I was looking at. It was a metate, a tool the Antelope Creek People relied on more than a thousand years ago for grinding corn and seed. Like the quarries on the nearby hills, the stone artifact was mute evidence of a vibrant culture, one of skilled men and women who lived, died, and disappeared long ago.

I walked over to the river, the banks lined with yellowed marsh grass, the water flowing gently toward a distant mesa. I saw no one, heard no one. A hawk soared in the azure sky.

SAN FELIPE DE AUSTIN WAS ONCE THE VITAL HEART OF TEXAS

SAN FELIPE DE AUSTIN

Heading west on I-10 out of Houston, you normally clear the clotted traffic at about the Fort Bend County line, if you're lucky; a few miles farther on you'll come to exit 723. A left turn at the Shell station will take you to Frydek, a tiny Czech farming community that's known for its historic Catholic church. A right turn takes you into a scattering of comfortable ranch-style houses set among lush green pastureland, along with a handful of weathered structures from the nineteenth century, a volunteer fire department, a front-yard barbecue stand, a few trucking businesses, and a couple of churches. Locals tend to call their small incorporated community San Phillip.

San Felipe or San Phillip, whatever your choice, is more than just a Sealy suburb. The historic hamlet was home to the Father of Texas, Stephen F. Austin, and the seat of Texas government for most of the Texas Revolution. If your detour into San Felipe were to take you into a time warp, you'd likely encounter everybody who was anybody in early Texas—Austin, of course, but also William Barret Travis, Gail Borden, Jane Long, Noah Smithwick, Angelina Peyton, and Judge Robert M. "Three-Legged Willie" Williamson. (His two-story wood-frame home, thought to have been built in 1836, still stands.)

Because of its vital role in the settlement of Texas and the push toward independence, this town on the west bank of the Brazos should be as prominent as Gonzales, Goliad, and Washington-on-the-Brazos. And yet it's been a long time since San Felipe has been anything more than a quiet community, its place in Texas history marked only by an obelisk and an Austin statue commissioned for the 1936 centennial.

Fortunately, San Felipe's obscurity may be changing. The recent opening of the handsome San Felipe de Austin museum is beginning to draw visitors in numbers the historic site deserves.

"We're here to tell a story that's mainly forgotten and is subtler than the Battle of the Alamo or the Battle of San Jacinto," site manager Bryan McAuley told me.

It's subtler because San Felipe is not about battlefield exploits but about politics and intense planning for a different type of Texas—either a separate Mexican state or an independent republic. The San Felipe story is about Texans sitting around a table arguing, debating, and plotting as events rush inexorably toward some kind of confrontation with the tumultuous Mexican government.

The town came into being in 1823 as the capital of Austin's colony. The empresario envisioned a town with a regular grid of avenues and four Spanish-style public plazas, similar to towns he had encountered on his journey to Mexico City in 1822. As it turned out, the settlement grew more aimlessly, sprawling westward from the Brazos for more than half a mile along Atascosito Road (FM 1458).

"Austin seemed to think that all of his settlers would live close to him in a city, like Mexico City," McAuley said. The colonists, though, preferred living on their land grants away from the village proper.

With about six hundred people at its peak, San Felipe soon became the second largest settlement in Texas, behind San Antonio. It was home to several taverns that provided meals and public accommodations, three hotels, a billiard hall, merchants, a livery stable, two blacksmith shops, Austin's home and land office, and the first consistently published newspaper in Texas, the *Texas Gazette*, under the editorship of Godwin B. Cotten. A second newspaper in town, Gail Borden's *Telegraph and Texas Register*, edited for a time by Williamson (he of three legs), became the unofficial journal of the revolution.

Regular mail service in the colony started in 1826 when Samuel May Williams was appointed postmaster in San Felipe; seven separate postal routes converged at San Felipe until the revolution. By 1836 at least three steamboats were plying the Brazos between San Felipe and the coast, eighty miles to the southeast.

The thriving town hosted the vital Conventions of 1832 and 1833 and served as the capital of the provisional government until the Convention of 1836 met the following March at nearby Washington-on-the-Brazos.

After the fall of the Alamo, Gen. Sam Houston's dispirited army tramped through San Felipe and headed eastward toward the Sabine. Houston left behind a small garrison under Moseley Baker to defend the Brazos crossing. On March 30, 1836, Baker ordered the town evacuated and then burned it to the ground to keep it from falling into the hands of the advancing Mexican army.

"By sunset we could make out some truncated pyramids that turned out to be the chimneys of houses in what had been the township of San Felipe," José Enrique de la Peña, a colonel in Santa Anna's army, wrote in his journal on April 14, 1836. "The fruits of many years of hard work had been destroyed in one moment of madness."

There may have been method to the madness, McAuley suggests. "The Brazos became Santa Anna's chief obstacle," he said, "and the three days they twiddled here may have been what kept him from capturing the Republic's government at Harrisburg."

A bronze sculpture at the new museum by Navasota artist J. Payne Lara commemorates the terrified residents of San Felipe who hastily gathered up what few belongings they could carry and fled eastward during the Runaway Scrape. Many, but not all, began returning after the Battle of San Jacinto, but their town never regained its early prominence. When the railroad picked Sealy in the mid-1870s, San Felipe gradually settled into rural somnolence.

The ten-thousand-square-foot museum, airy and high-ceilinged and featuring the latest interactive technology, brings those early decades back to life. A large touch-screen wall mural depicts an interactive layout of San Felipe's downtown prior to independence. Visitors can engage with its stories by touching animations on the large screen. The museum's permanent collection includes a desk that once belonged to Austin, a cast-iron printing press like the one used to publish Travis's "Victory or Death" letter, and hundreds of artifacts recovered during archaeological digs at the state historic site. The largest exhibit is an 1830s-era log cabin from the Columbus area that was rebuilt inside the museum.

"Our hope is that visitors come here and learn what they didn't know before," McAuley said, as he stood before the interactive mural.

I'm guessing they will. They'll come away knowing more about Angelina Peyton (tavern keeper and heroine of the "Archives War"), the amazing Gail Borden (the milkman), and, of course, esteemed editor, soldier, lawyer, and judge Robert McAlpin Williamson, who wore a wooden leg to compensate for a right leg drawn back at the knee as the result of a childhood illness (thus, "Three-Legged Willie").

OLD AND LOST ARE MUSIC
TO A NATURE LOVER'S EARS

OLD RIVER-WINFREE

L ike many southeast Texans, I've driven by the road signs count-
less times over the years, the signs on I-10 near Baytown that
mark a bridge over OLD AND LOST RIVER for eastbound traffic,
and LOST AND OLD RIVER for westbound. I know now that "river"
ought to be plural since we're talking about two Trinity River tributaries instead of one.

Nevertheless, there's something evocative about the phrase, sin-
gular or plural, eastbound or west—so evocative that it inspired a
haunting orchestral work. I could be wrong, but I know of no other
road sign that can make such a claim.

In 1986 New York composer Tobias Picker was working as
composer-in-residence with the Houston Symphony. Preparing
new music for the symphony's celebration of the Texas sesqui-
centennial, he happened to notice the I-10 sign as he drove eastward. His work "Old and Lost Rivers" premiered in Jones Hall on
May 9, 1986.

"It is obviously an extremely poetic phrase," Picker told the
Houston Chronicle years later. "It is just full of meaning and impli-
cations and symbolism. It can mean many things to many people if
you think about it."

I recently decided to explore the meanings and symbolism for myself in the company of my *Chronicle* friend Shannon Tompkins. The veteran columnist not only happens to be the best and most knowledgeable outdoors writer in Texas (and beyond); he was also born and raised in the area.

"A college-educated swamp creature who spends most of his life outdoors" (to quote the late Gary Cartwright of *Texas Monthly*), Shannon has hunted, fished, trapped, and roamed the sloughs, rivers, and bayous of Chambers County his whole life. Halfway between Houston and Beaumont, within sight and rumbling sound of I-10, this green and marshy land is perfect for a devoted outdoorsman. It boasts more than its share of rich historic lore, abundant wildlife, and bounteous bird species.

Lost River is an old channel of the lower Trinity, abandoned by the restless river before the area was settled. The tree-lined Old River, also an abandoned channel, begins in Liberty County and flows southeasterly to Old River Lake and ultimately into Trinity Bay.

As we meandered along country roads in Shannon's Ford F-150 pickup (a 2004 model with 353,000 miles on it), passing through verdant coastal prairie populated by great egrets and roseate spoonbills, white-faced ibis and green herons, and, of course, alligators, he reminded me that we were in Faulkner country.

"Once you learn the old families, it's Old South more than anything else," he said.

As in Faulkner's fictional Yoknapatawpha County, many of the original families have white and Black branches. I learned about one still-prominent family who divvied up the land between Black and white in the early 1900s; the Black family members received the swampland portion. As fate—or geology—would have it, these descendants of enslaved people turned out to be proprietors of the oil-rich portion of the original family holdings. ("God has a sense of humor," Chambers County Museum administrator Marie Hughes said.)

True to its Old South traditions, the area tolerated the Ku Klux Klan both during Reconstruction and in the 1920s, when Prohibition and anti-immigrant sentiments roiled the populace. As one local historian suggested a few years ago, the masked avengers were merely a gallant group of guys employing "corrective measures" to keep the peace. (The Cuban barber at Mont Belvieu they ran out of town or the many others they bullied and mistreated no doubt thought differently.)

Long before transplanted southerners moved into the area, this was Spanish country. Near present-day Wallisville in 1756, two Franciscan missionaries established Mission Nuestra Señora de la Luz to minister to members of the Orcoquiza and Bidai tribes. A contingent of thirty Spanish soldiers built San Agustín de Ahumada a mile away to guard against French encroachment from the east. The state historical marker near the Chambers County Museum describes the mission and fort as "two of the most misfortune-ridden outposts of Spain in Texas."

The elder of the two friars died soon after arrival, and the younger complained of ravenous insects, extremes of heat and cold, and "thick and stinking water" in the lake near the lonely mission. The soldiers were ill-prepared, the fifty families who were to establish a town never showed up, and the Natives were restless. By 1771 the Spanish were gone.

The pirate Jean Lafitte nosed about the neighborhood—two of his ships are said to be buried in the mud of Lake Charlotte—and hotheaded Texans in and around nearby Anahuac plotted rebellion against Mexico. Other things have happened as well, as I learned at the superb county museum.

I learned about the Dick Disturbance, an 1880s-era cattle-rustling scandal that began when John Dick, a former British army officer, moved into the area with his twelve children. His boys were desperadoes and thieves. "Everybody was afraid of them, because they always rode in a bunch armed with .44 caliber Winchester rifles and six-shooters," early settler Forest W. McNeir wrote in a 1956 memoir.

When Sarah Ridge Pix, a former Cherokee princess, discovered altered brands on her cattle and other ranchers noticed that they were losing animals, two of the Dick sons, George and Benajah (known as Ninny), became prime suspects. Suspicions were confirmed when the Chambers County sheriff and his posse discovered a freshly slaughtered bull and green hides in the hull of the Dick family's sloop.

I also learned about the Hog War. In December 1906 Wallisville civic leaders sought to prevent domestic and feral hogs from making their regular winter migration into town to feast on garbage strewn about the courthouse lawn. The proposal requiring hog farmers to keep their animals penned was approved by three votes, but the hog farmers managed to channel opposition to the new law into efforts to move the courthouse to Anahuac. A referendum to that effect passed in 1907, and Wallisville lost its courthouse to the upstart across Turtle Bay.

"We have spits and spats still," said Joe Landry, mayor of Old River-Winfree for the past twenty-five years, but nothing like the old days. For Landry and other elected officials, the challenge is keeping up with rampant growth. Once rural and largely undeveloped, this coastal prairie dotted with small communities is rapidly giving way to suburban sprawl.

Not completely, though, as my friend showed me. Still lingering, at least for a while, are snowy egrets with bright yellow feet and majestic green herons and ducks of every variety. Still lingering are mysterious cypress swamps and shawls of Spanish moss and brilliant-green water plants and pinkish-white marshmallow flowers, as well as raccoons and muskrats and yellow-eyed gators gliding through clusters of water hyacinths. Still lingering are coffee-colored streams, Old and Lost, where birdcalls echo among the tall pines and cypresses, where a busy interstate and massive chemical plants and subdivisions spreading amoebalike across the prairie seem far away. At least for a little while.

STILL QUIET AND PEACEFUL
ON JOHN GRAVES'S BRAZOS

GRAFORD

I'd never say so out loud, but I've always thought of myself as a "manly man"—ballplayer as a kid, sports fan, willing to get down and dirty when there's hard physical work to do—until recently when I finally had to admit I'd been fooling myself. I came to that rueful awareness when my wife, Laura, and I were strolling by a bookstore next door to an REI, and I found myself tending like a wayward canoe toward the bookstore.

Laura had to reorient me, knowing that I needed gear for a three-day canoe trip with three friends down the upper-middle Brazos River in Palo Pinto County, near Mineral Wells. On my shopping list were a hat, a bedroll, and pants that would shed water, since I'd probably end up in the river at some point.

Did I mention that I'm not an outdoorsman? I had last wielded a paddle a couple of years earlier when Laura and I joined former Houston mayor Bill White, his wife Andrea, and several mutual friends on a leisurely afternoon kayaking trek down Buffalo Bayou. Not long after we got on the water at the Dunlavy, rounding the bend just beyond the Wortham, Laura glanced over her shoulder with a question: "Are you sure you're paddling back there?"

The Brazos trip was a literary homage of sorts to a Texas writer all four of us admired. In November 1957 the late John Graves, accompanied by a six-month-old dachshund named Passenger, spent three weeks canoeing the stretch of river we were on, 150 curlicued miles between Possum Kingdom Dam and the upper reaches of Lake Whitney. Graves's account of that trip, *Goodbye to a River*, is generally considered among the three or four best books ever written by a Texan.

Georgetown resident Sam Pfiester organized the trip and served as camp cook and guide. A retired oilman who spent a major portion of his career in Midland as an associate of oil-and-gas magnate (and gubernatorial candidate) Clayton Williams, Pfiester is a writer and more recently a movie producer whose latest project features a plucky chicken named Blanche. An outdoorsman who has paddled rivers all over the world, he was good-humored about his companions' camping ineptitude.

In addition to a journalist more comfortable with pen than paddle, Pfiester was stuck with my old friend Mark Busby, a retired professor of southwestern literature at Texas State University and the author of a literary biography of Graves, and Steve Davis, the congenial curator of the Wittliff Southwestern Writers Collection at Texas State. The collection Steve oversees is home to Graves's papers and memorabilia, including the paddle he used for his trip down the Brazos. The three of us did our best to repay the ever-curious Sam by sharing stories about the quiet, self-effacing man who wrote so winningly about history, nature, country life, and Texas lore.

We were surprised by the relative emptiness of so-called Palo Pinto country. (The name shared by the county, the tiny county seat, and the general area means "painted stick.") The river runs through it.

"When you paddle and pole along it," Graves wrote more than six decades ago, "the things you see are much the same things the

Comanches and the Kiowas used to see, riding lean ponies down it a hundred years ago to raid the new settlements in its valley."

It's still that way. We floated past a Boy Scout camp and maybe four houses in the wooded hills along the twenty-mile stretch of river.

Graves in 1957 thought he was seeing the Brazos for the last time in its natural state, knowing that the U.S. Army Corps of Engineers was set to tame the occasionally raucous river with a series of dams. He could imagine what was coming. Like the Highland Lakes on the Colorado, the placid bodies of water behind the dams would attract noisy boaters and skiers; second homes and condos would crowd traffic-choked shores.

The dams were never built, in part because of the eloquent persuasiveness of *Goodbye to a River*. The river still flows between castellated sandstone bluffs and past giant rhombic blocks, the stream bending like a giant's bobby pin between cedar-draped hills, the dark-green foliage complemented in spring days by newly leafed oaks as bright green as Bibb lettuce. Glancing down as we paddled, we could see "stone by stone," as Graves noted long ago, "the texture of the bottom as it slid past."

Occasionally Graves crunched the canoe's bow into a sandbar, stepped ashore with stumpy-legged Passenger at his heels, and visited with an old farmer, a fisherman, or a storekeeper in an isolated community near the river. In our three days on the water we visited with no one. We saw a total of four people—three in one motorboat headed upriver, one in another. They waved but didn't tarry. Except for our own voices, the sluicing sound of shallow water over rocks, and the antic yips of coyotes at night, it was quiet in the heart of Texas.

Graves communed with other river denizens as well—with ghosts of settlers from the century preceding who had pushed their luck farming and raising a family on the raw farthest edge of frontier safety, and with Comanches and Kiowas, their eons-old way of life inexorably being eradicated.

He told about Jesse Veale, the last man killed by Indians in Palo Pinto County. One afternoon in 1873, young Jesse and his buddy Joe Corbin were setting fishlines in the river when they ran across saddled Indian ponies staked out in the cedars. The young men took them.

At Ioni Creek the next morning, two Comanches caught up with them. An arrow bore into Jesse's knee; his horse went to bucking. Joe yelled, "What the hell we gonna do?"

He thought Jesse yelled, "Run it out!" and so he did. "When he last looked back (how many times did he see it again, the rest of his life, how many times did he wonder if what Jesse Veale had said was: 'Fight it out'?), Jesse was on the ground shooting and clubbing with his pistol, and they were all over him."

The only stories we heard—except for those we told each other—were from outfitter Bud Rochelle as he drove us in his pickup to the put-in place. His stories were tamer. An ex-navy man in a sleeveless T-shirt whose beefy arms made me wonder whether he had pulled oars on a Roman galley, Rochelle grew up in Houston but decamped to the family outfitting business in 1980. His grandfather had started Rochelle's Canoe Rental in 1969.

He told us about the eight-months-pregnant woman who insisted on an overnight trip. You can guess what happened; she named the baby Brazos. And there was the Metroplex fellow who didn't trust Rochelle with the keys to his brand-new pickup, despite his wife's advice to leave them on the keyboard in the office. The fellow didn't expect a raccoon to make off in the middle of the night with a Tupperware bowl, truck keys inside.

We saw tracks around our camp but no raccoons. We did see birds—great blue herons and ring-necked ducks, snowy egrets and a flock of black vultures, a woodpecker hard at work on the trunk of a dead tree, his tap-tap-tapping echoing through the woods. We saw an osprey poised midair above the water, his osprey eye homed in on a fish below the surface.

Mark and I tumped over only once. Somewhere near Chick Bend, we miscalculated shallow rapids looping around an island and rammed into the exposed roots of a tree on the bank. The last I saw of my new hat, it was bobbing down the river far beyond us.

THE LINE AT THE BORDER
DOESN'T ALWAYS DIVIDE

MARATHON

Glance at a map of North America, and you'll notice a precise dark line designating a nearly two-thousand-mile border dividing two nations, Mexico and the United States. Residents in the vicinity of that line, on both sides, know that the map misleads. In real life, the demarcation is actually a watercolor stroke smudging into the paper, spreading in both directions. Border life merges, and has for centuries.

I got to thinking about lines and smudges and international borders during a lively conversation with my friend Lloyd, a third-generation rancher whose ten-thousand-acre spread borders the Rio Grande between Del Rio and Big Bend National Park. Lloyd—a pseudonym for reasons that will soon become clear—is a living, breathing symbol of the complexities and contradictions of the U.S.–Mexico border, complexities and contradictions that rarely make their way into public policy.

A Weller whiskey aficionado and boisterous storyteller, Lloyd is a big, buff former college football star who scored a tryout with the Houston Oilers in the late 1970s. He's also a husband and father and a local elected official. A Trump supporter—"Trump made me a lot of money," he says—he's fluent in Spanish. Although he knows and respects his neighbors across the river, he supports a border wall, not for the rugged Big Bend region where he's lived all his life but through flat, easy-to-cross farmland in the Rio Grande Valley and across the New Mexico–Arizona desert portion of the border.

Like other Big Bend–area ranchers, including his nearest neighbor twenty miles to the east, he's accustomed to undocumented travelers knocking on his door. He tells me they've become even more numerous since Joe Biden was elected president. They have never caused problems.

Lloyd's cliff-top ranch house, built of native stone and commanding stunning mountain views of Mexico's Maderas del Carmen, is thirty miles off the nearest paved road. To get anywhere near the house and nearby casitas, undocumented immigrants headed north must traverse rugged, rocky peaks and steep-walled gorges. If it's summer, a relentless Chihuahuan Desert sun is a punishing reminder that if they run out of water, they're in big trouble. Looking around, they'll see that every piece of vegetation that has managed to survive in such forbidding terrain is armed with formidable thorns. Almost every creature, no matter how small, either bites or stings.

Still, they come. Not long ago a half-dozen or so young men showed up. Lloyd could tell by their accents they weren't Mexican. By their clothes, he guessed they were Central American, city dwellers most likely.

"Can you guys lay tile?" he asked. "Pour concrete? Fix fences?"

Each question elicited a shake of the head. Something about them—maybe their tattoos—made him uneasy. He gave them water and food and sent them along.

A man and woman showed up at Lloyd's door on a cold, dark night last winter. "My wife is sick," the man said, a worried look on his face, his voice shaky. "Can you help me get her to a doctor?"

Lloyd could tell she was seriously ill, maybe with Covid, maybe something else. He also knew he couldn't get them to town without passing the Border Patrol checkpoint. He decided to load them into his truck and take them along a gravel road to the crossing at Boquillas, the Mexican village across from the national park. He knew there was a clinic there.

A couple of hours later he dropped off the couple at river's edge. They waded into the water, cold and waist deep. Suddenly a national park ranger—not a Border Patrol officer—popped up from a stand of tall cane where he had been hiding. He called them back and arrested them.

Lloyd was enraged. "You chickensh—!" he yelled. "She's sick. They were headed back!"

Lloyd has cameras situated near the house and at various locations around the sprawling ranch. One day he was in Del Rio when a camera activated a signal on his smartphone. Calling up the camera image, he saw a gray-haired man, shirtless and obviously addled. He was staggering around in circles.

Lloyd called him on his phone. The man, who must have thought God was speaking to him, looked up toward the sky. "Stay right there," Lloyd told him. "I'll be there in a couple of hours."

The man's name was Efraim. He told Lloyd he had been with a group trudging through the desert with a coyote they had paid to guide them. Older than most in the group and out of shape, he fell behind shortly after their guide got them into Texas. He watched Border Patrol agents apprehend them all. Desperate, with no idea where he was, he waved his arms and yelled. He wanted to be arrested too, but no one heard his cries.

Efraim's feet were a bubbly mass of painful blisters. Lloyd treated them, found him some clean clothes, and told him to stay around the house for a few days until he recuperated.

Efraim admitted that he was returning to the United States and said that he had worked in Atlanta for several years operating a ditch-digging machine for a cable company. He and his wife got into an argument, he said. The police came. He got deported.

As Lloyd tells the story, he looks Efraim in the eye and demands the truth. "If you're a wife beater," he told him, "I'll find out. The Border Patrol will be out here quick as I can call 'em."

"No, no," Efraim pleaded. "It was just an argument, a little mis-understanding. We couldn't make the police understand."

He gave Lloyd phone numbers for his now-former wife and their grown daughters. They attested to his good character. Lloyd was satisfied that Efraim was a good man. Unlike the Central Americans, he could lay tile, pour concrete, and repair fences. He ended up staying at the ranch for three months.

On a day when the checkpoint was closed, Efraim managed to make his way to Austin. Friends drove him to Orlando, Florida, where his daughters lived. He found a job. He's still there today. He and Lloyd stay in touch.

"Borders blend," Lloyd tells me, taking a swig from his nearly empty bottle of Weller special reserve. So does whiskey. And people.

Texas, *My* Texas

When asked, as I have been very often,
to explain what I love about Texas,
given all that I know of what has happened there—
and is still happening there—
the best response I can give is this is where
my first family and connections were.

— ANNETTE GORDON-REED,
On Juneteenth

THE FOLK HERO OL' BIGFOOT WALLACE

AUSTIN

On Monument Hill, a beautiful state park on the outskirts of La Grange, is a forty-eight-foot-tall cenotaph erected in 1936, the Texas centennial year. The impressive monument at the edge of a high bluff above the Colorado River towers above a granite burial vault containing the bones of Texans who died during the ill-fated Dawson and Mier expeditions in 1842 and 1843. The bones were collected in Mexico in 1848.

The names inscribed on two sides of the monument recognize those men who volunteered to take up arms and drive off Mexican armies that kept messing with Texas post–San Jacinto. Among the names is one William Alexander Anderson Wallace, better known as Bigfoot. The Indian fighter, Texas Ranger, and quintessential frontiersman survived the bloody battle at the border town of Mier, drew a lifesaving white bean as part of the notorious black bean massacre a few weeks later, and endured two years of maltreatment in a cold, dank Mexican prison called Perote.

I've had something of a family interest in ol' Bigfoot, largely because my mother grew up in the Frio County village that bears his name. My grandmother ran Bigfoot's only general store, and in the 1950s she flew to New York and stumped an NBC-TV quiz show panel trying to guess the name of her hometown. The panel guessed "Big Feet," not Bigfoot, so Mammy came home with prize money in her purse.

Something else about Bigfoot Wallace interests me. He's one of those frontier characters whose long, colorful lives bleed into legend. A folk hero, a Texan Pecos Bill of sorts, he probably represents the quintessential Texan (for good or ill).

That's what Robert Howard thought. The eccentric creator of Conan the Barbarian—who grew up in Cross Plains, by the way—labeled Bigfoot "the greatest figure in Southwestern legendary."

Bigfoot inspired stories and tall tales, even during his lifetime. Bud Shrake, Larry McMurtry, and other Texas writers have worked him into novels and screenplays. Bob Thompson, author of a book about the transformation of Tennessee congressman David Crockett into Davy Crockett, "king of the wild frontier," writes that when Walt Disney's team put together a tentative list of historical characters to feature in a TV series about the frontier, the list included Crockett, Daniel Boone, Johnny Appleseed, and Bigfoot Wallace.

Not long ago, I dropped by the Dolph Briscoe Center for American History at the University of Texas to investigate the real Bigfoot, the man behind the legend. Among letters, photographs, and personal memorabilia in the Bigfoot Wallace collection, I got to see—but not touch—a buckskin coat he wore. The fringed garment is stored in a large cardboard box, a container you might use for a valuable mink coat. Family lore has it that he left it with relatives in Lexington, Virginia, where he grew up, in 1859.

Bigfoot's letters home, the handwriting as graceful as a missive from one of the Founding Fathers, reveal a surprisingly literate man, an astute observer of life in early Texas.

He got to Texas in 1837 as a nineteen-year-old, hoping to avenge the death of a brother and a cousin who had fallen at Goliad. Landing in Galveston in November of that year, he made his way to Houston a few weeks later. As he wrote to his father in a letter dated December 26, he was less than impressed with the Allen brothers' scruffy little settlement on the bayou or with Texas in general.

"I have seen a great many families here that want to get back to the States but cannot get back," he wrote. "And well they might for the Indians scalp them from the mountains to the Gulf, and have beat the rangers in every attempt. And worse society could not be found on the globe. People here kill each other every day. People in Texas die like rotten sheep. The City of Houston contains about three thousand inhabitants, which ten months ago there was not a house in the place. And I will venture to say that there is three times the number of graves around Houston than there is in the graveyard at Lexington, VA."

Despite his initial disdain, Bigfoot stayed in Texas, eventually making his way to the new state capital being hacked out of the wilderness on the banks of the Colorado. In Austin he dug wells, worked on construction projects, and provided meat for the growing town. He also rode with local citizens on the trail of Comanche raiding parties.

During the Mexican War, Bigfoot served with the Texas Rangers under Capt. Jack Hays and during the Civil War guarded the Texas frontier as a private in a Confederate unit (despite being opposed to secession).

One of the stories I came across in the Briscoe collection recounted one of his Civil War misadventures. In a letter to a family friend in Virginia, he recalled being on a nighttime scouting mission with two other soldiers. Indians attacked, stampeding the trio's horses and killing Bigfoot's two companions. Bigfoot escaped into the darkness with only the clothes on his back, his revolver, and a Bowie knife.

Trying to reach a pool of water the next morning, he fell down a rocky ravine and broke his left leg. Miles from the fort and in rough terrain, he realized he was in a fix. Accustomed to making do, he noticed wet clay at the edge of the pool. Crawling to the mud, he tore his shirt into strips, bound his broken leg tightly, and used the clay as a thick mud-plaster cast, keeping the leg as still as possible.

On the twenty-first day, he removed the plaster and discovered, "to my great joy," that the bones were bound back together. He found that by using a forked stick as a crutch, he could slowly and cautiously walk. Tiring, he lay down under a rock shelf and fell into a fitful sleep. The howling of what he called a "coyote wolf" only a few yards away startled him awake.

"I took as deliberative aim at him with my revolver as my nervous and exhausted condition permitted," Bigfoot recalled, "and blazed away, providentially killing him; then I cut his throat and sucked his blood until I had swallowed a pint or more, when I was compelled to stop by violent cramps in my stomach. After suffering untold agonies for an hour or more, the pain gradually subsided, and I fell into a sound and refreshing slumber. This was the first food that had been in my stomach for twenty-one days."

Late that night Bigfoot awoke with "an insatiable desire" to eat the raw flesh of the wolf. Afraid it might kill him, he partially relieved his cravings by chewing on the flesh and only swallowing the juice. The next morning he built a fire and roasted the hams of the wolf for sustenance and then walked for two days back to the fort, "where I was received as one of the dead."

True, false, or maybe partially true, Bigfoot frontier stories abound. Folklorist J. Frank Dobie had this to say about the tale-teller, writing in the *Handbook of Texas:* "He was a mellow and convivial soul who liked to sit in a roomy rawhide-bottomed chair in the shade of his shanty and tell over the stories of his career. . . . Wallace was as honest as daylight but liked to stretch the blanket and embroider his stories."

As a kid I liked to sit on the front porch of my grandmother's store not far from where Bigfoot's cabin had been and listen to stories the old-timers told each other, old-timers who may have known Bigfoot. I'm guessing they stretched the blanket too. I didn't know, didn't care. I liked listening.

Across the road from the store was the Bigfoot Post Office, presided over by longtime postmistress Lizzie Thomas, my grandmother's lifelong friend.

When Lizzie was a girl, her folks took care of ol' Bigfoot. By then he had developed tremors so severe he had to bind his wrist to the kitchen table with a leather strap in order to eat. He blamed his condition on the ill treatment he endured decades earlier at Perote, the Mexican prison.

Bigfoot died of pneumonia in 1899 and was laid to rest in a cemetery near the village that bore his name. He was eighty-two. Not long afterward, the Texas Legislature appropriated funds to move his body to the state cemetery in Austin. The gravestone bears this simple epitaph:

BIG FOOT WALLACE
Here Lies He Who Spent His Manhood
Defending the Homes of Texas
Brave Honest and Faithful

A BRUSH WITH BONNIE AND CLYDE'S GETAWAY DRIVERS

HILLSBORO

Under a metallic-gray sky on a winter afternoon in the early 1930s, a young man with a double-barreled shotgun in the crook of his right arm trudged through a post oak thicket. He was a mile or so from the small farmhouse where he and his wife and two children lived. A boy, scuffing through fallen leaves, trailed a couple of steps behind his dad. The youngster, his cheeks red from the cold, wore a corduroy cap, the flaps covering his ears.

The two were hungry, as were the wife and girl back at the house. Twice the man scared up a squirrel; twice he fired. And missed. With no more shells, he and his son turned toward home.

Late that night the young husband and father, desperate to feed his family, went out hunting again on a neighboring farm. This time he was more successful, although success came at a price. As court records show, he was found guilty "of the offense of the theft of one chicken." The court decreed punishment "by confinement in the jail for a term of one hundred days."

The young man who served time in the Hill County jail was my uncle; I'm his namesake. I read the court documents during my recent visit to this pleasant Central Texas town.

One of Joe's cellmates was a young punk from West Dallas named Raymond Hamilton. Already a hardened criminal at age twenty, Hamilton and his older brother, Floyd, were drivers for Bonnie Parker and Clyde Barrow. One writer has remarked that the Hamilton boys could drive like hell and were afraid of nothing.

The younger Hamilton was behind bars for the 1932 murder of John N. Bucher, a Hillsboro jeweler and optician, during a burglary attempt gone awry. Even though Hamilton had been in Michigan at the time of the murder, a Hill County jury found him guilty but couldn't agree on his sentence, so the judge declared a mistrial. He was in jail awaiting a new trial.

On March 21 Hamilton and two other men escaped. Family lore has it that a deputy sheriff brought a group of students upstairs to the second-floor cells on a tour of the jail. Hamilton got the jump on the deputy, grabbed his gun, and asked Joe if he wanted to come along. "Thanks, but no thanks," he said, or something to that effect.

Hamilton, five feet three inches tall and not yet twenty-one, led the students back down the stairs as if he were conducting the tour. He and his cohorts ran across the street to a gas station, stole a car, and headed out of town. Or so the story goes.

Dick McMahan, a resident of nearby Whitney and the author of *The Bucher Murder Was the Turning Point for Clyde Barrow, Bonnie Parker, and Raymond Hamilton*, tells what is probably the more accurate story. He writes that Hamilton and two other inmates slipped in behind two deputies who were bringing another prisoner to his cell, took their weapons and keys, and clattered down the stairs to freedom.

Armed with a .30-30 Winchester and a twelve-gauge shotgun, the trio hurried across the street to a gas station and stole a car belonging to Mrs. Beatrice Hare. About twelve miles west of Hillsboro, the car blew a tire, the law caught up with the escapees, and they surrendered. They were unaware that Hare had brought her car in to have the tire looked at.

Hamilton and friends were free for about an hour and a half. "No harm was done to anyone and we were just having some fun," the so-called Depression Desperado told the *Hillsboro Mirror*.

On June 2, 1933, Raymond Hamilton was found guilty of the Bucher murder and sentenced to life in prison. In January 1934 he and four other inmates fled the notorious Eastham Prison Farm in a daring scheme engineered by Clyde, Bonnie, and brother Floyd, who were waiting in a nearby car. One of the escapees shot and killed a prison guard.

Recaptured in Lewisville five months later, Raymond Hamilton was tried and sentenced to death. In January 1934 he escaped again, this time from death row. He was on the lam for nine months before being recaptured in Dallas County. By then Bonnie and Clyde were dead, shot to pieces in a law enforcement ambush in rural Louisiana.

Raymond Hamilton went to the electric chair on May 10, 1935. His last words were "Well, goodbye all." He was twenty-two.

Joe, my uncle, served his hundred days, left the farm for other lines of work, and in 1934 received a pardon from Gov. Miriam "Ma" Ferguson. His pardon was one of several thousand she granted to Texans convicted of such minor Depression-era crimes as small-time bootlegging and chicken-thieving. The old yellow-brick jail where he served his hundred days still exists. It's now the Hill County Cell Block Museum.

Not long after Raymond Hamilton's execution, Floyd went on a bank-robbing spree in the Midwest and was declared public enemy no. 1. He spent time in Leavenworth and in Alcatraz, where he lived in a cell next to the legendary "Birdman," Robert Stroud. In 1943 he escaped. Wet and cold, he holed up in a shoreline cave for two days before surrendering. He then spent nine years in solitary confinement.

Released from prison in 1958, Floyd returned to Dallas, caught on as a night watchman for a Dallas car dealer—former Dallas County sheriff Bill Decker vouched for him—and lived a quiet life in the West Dallas neighborhood where he and Raymond had grown up. (West Dallas, a tough neighborhood then and now, was also known as the Devil's Back Porch.)

One afternoon in the late 1970s I knocked on the front door of a small frame house in West Dallas. An elderly man with a fringe of white hair peered through the screen door. When I told him I was a reporter, he invited me in.

We sat in the dimly lit living room, and I asked Floyd Hamilton if he would consent to an interview. "Well, maybe," he said. "Why don't you call me back in about a week, and I'll let you know."

When I called, Hamilton was not happy. Since we had talked, he had consented to an interview with a young reporter from one of the Dallas papers. He was telling her about hard times in solitary and how he developed pyorrhea, a dental disease. She heard another word, one that rhymes with pyorrhea, and that's what she went with in her story. "I'll never talk to another reporter again," he told me over the phone.

Floyd Hamilton died in 1984. Whether he kept his word about reporters, I cannot say. I know he didn't talk to me.

WHAT HAPPENED IN MISS HATTIE'S PARLOR

SAN ANGELO

Walking up the dimly lit stairs to Miss Hattie's Parlor on a recent weekday afternoon, my mind was on my previous visit to San Angelo's best-known bordello. That time—my first time—my dad was with me. And I nearly killed him.

Here's what happened. Fifteen years ago my dad was in his early nineties, and with his memory flaking away like paint on an old house, I wanted to hear, perhaps for the last time, the stories I had grown up listening to about his youth on a Hill County farm and his wanderings throughout the 1920s when he hopped freight trains and followed the wheat harvest northward. As a young man, he spent a lot of time in wide-open San Angelo with his uncle Joe, a larger-than-life fellow with a booming laugh and backslapping nature, who also was a bootlegger and big-time gambler. I wanted to hear those stories too, so on a weekday morning before the sun's rise I picked up my dad in Waco, and we headed west.

He was seventeen or eighteen, he told me, when he first started taking the train to San Angelo. His mother's brother, footloose Joe Cochran, had drifted in to San Angelo in 1910. Joe stayed, perhaps because the town was bigger spirited, roomier than rural Central Texas where he grew up and was able to tolerate a young hell-raiser.

Everybody liked Joe, my grandfather once told me, but he couldn't stay out of trouble.

By the time my dad started going to San Angelo in the 1920s, his uncle had built a respectable life, on the surface at least. He owned rent houses and ran the concession service at the Elks Club. Joe, his wife, and their two daughters lived in a comfortable white frame house in a quiet neighborhood on East Ninth.

On weekday mornings Uncle Joe would dress, always in a white suit, and go downtown. Sometimes he drove by the house in the middle of the afternoon and honked his horn, and my dad would accompany him on what he called "his rounds"—collecting rent on the houses he owned.

Riding in Joe Cochran's Model T Ford was unsettling at first, my dad recalled, because the seat rested directly on the floorboard. Joe had removed the springs and supports so he could squeeze his six-foot-four-inch, three-hundred-pound frame under the steering wheel; a passenger found himself nearly on the floor, legs straight out in front, barely able to see over the dashboard. My dad soon learned to take a pillow.

Occasionally Joe took him downtown to the Elks Lodge. Walking with him along a crowded street, my dad noticed how he seemed to know everybody. He was Big Joe Cochran, and San Angelo was his town.

He also took my dad to the farm near Paint Rock where he had his still. One evening hogs had gotten into the sour mash and were staggering around drunk. "Uncle Joe liketa died laughing," my dad remembered.

Joe's partner in business was a woman named Hattie Foster, the widow of a Fort Concho army officer who not only owned property around town but also ran the most popular brothel in San Angelo. My dad remembered being with Joe on visits to Miss Hattie (at her residence, that is). She was tall, he remembered, with dark hair, and was always dressed like a lady.

On our San Angelo trip we were surprised to discover Miss Hattie's Parlor, a small bordello museum downtown on East Concho Street. The young woman who sold us our tickets told us that there were actually three Miss Hatties. The third was run out of town by the Texas Rangers in 1948 and resettled in South Austin; we decided my dad had known Miss Hattie no. 2.

We climbed the steep stairs to the second floor. The lamplit parlor at the top was furnished with a couple of Victorian sofas, a frayed Persian rug, and the obligatory upright piano. Off a long narrow hallway that ran to the back alley were small, windowless rooms behind screen doors, each one decorated according to the whims of the particular girl who conducted business in that room.

I was reading a Miss Hattie's employment application, my back to my dad, when I heard him fall. He must have been standing at the head of the steep stairs looking at a picture on the wall when he stepped back. Hearing the horrific clatter, I knew I had killed him—in a bordello, for Pete's sake.

He had come to rest on a landing, his head angled downward, his legs crumpled. Falling back the way he had, maybe even somersaulting, he should have broken his neck—certainly a hip—but as I knelt beside him I couldn't see any obvious injury. As he regained his senses, everything seemed to be in working order. "What happened?" he asked me a couple of times.

An emergency medical crew arrived within a few minutes. Four men clambered up the stairs to the landing, one carrying an orange padded board used to stabilize a person with head or neck injuries.

"What happened, sir?" one of the men asked.

My dad rolled his eyes toward me. "He pushed me," he said.

I knew he was joking—or rather I hoped he was—but the EMS men didn't know. They looked at me, I looked at them, and then—to my relief—he chuckled. He was embarrassed lying on the stairs with everyone staring down at him and was trying to relieve the tension.

"Wasn't me," I said. "I bet the ghost of Miss Hattie gave you a shove."

Walking up the stairs of Miss Hattie's Parlor more recently, I saw no ghosts, but I missed my dad, gone now for a decade. He and I went to a lot of places together over the years, although I'm not sure I could have persuaded him to climb those stairs again. A WATCH YOUR STEP sign is now glued to the bottom step.

THE DARK SKIES OF WACO
GIVE WAY TO SUNLIGHT

WACO

W hen I was a kid, eons ago, I'd spend summer mornings sprawled in the dirt beneath two backyard live oaks, busily building a town. I lined up cast-off bricks and propped foot-long "skyscraper" two-by-fours along palm-smoothed, dried-mud streets. I scraped out overpasses and platted highways leading to mountains in the distance (actually two piles of gravel that city maintenance crews had left beyond our backyard fence).

My town was at the mercy of frequent "tornadoes," twisters precipitated by spats with my younger brother Kenny. Discovering bricks scattered about and skyscrapers lying on their sides, I immediately became a storm chaser, but the towheaded little twister was usually too quick and squirmy to pin down.

Kenny and I knew real tornadoes. On a sultry Monday afternoon in May 1953, we sat cross-legged at the front screen door and watched what looked like mothballs drop from a darkly ominous, green-tinged sky. The frenetic balls bounced atop the wet spring grass, until suddenly the rain and hail stopped and everything got still (deathly still, people would say later). We didn't know until our dad got home from work that evening that a tornado had ripped the heart out of downtown Waco a couple of miles away, taking the lives of 114 people and injuring nearly 600.

Dillon Meek knows about building towns—real towns, that is—and he's heard about "the Tornado," as Wacoans to this day refer to the deadliest twister in Texas history. A Baylor Law School graduate who grew up on a cattle ranch near Edna in South Texas, Meek was Waco's thirty-eight-year-old mayor when we met in 2023.

Over lunch recently at George's Restaurant, a venerable Baylor-area hangout known for a two-fisted mug of beer called "the Big O," we talked about how the tornado was the beginning, not of a temporary bust similar to what Houston has endured off and on, but of a decades-long slough. An old town that, when I was growing up, rivaled Austin in population and prosperity, settled into a restless slumber. Only in the last dozen years or so, the mayor suggested, has recovery started to kick in for my hometown and his adopted one. The boyish-looking mayor is Baylor-Baptist earnest about ensuring that Waco's impressive revival continues.

Although the deadly storm devastated the city decades before the mayor was born, he's dealt with its stubborn, lingering effects as both a city council member and as mayor. Downtown disappeared just as businesses all over the country were fleeing to the suburbs. The storm, ironically, provided many business owners an excuse. Downtown Waco hollowed out.

Staid city officials decided to be uncharacteristically daring. Urban planning gurus persuaded them to transform Waco's main street, Austin Avenue, into a pedestrian-only mall. The unfortunate experiment lingered for nearly thirty years. By the time Waco brought it to an end, crickets in storefront doorways outnumbered pedestrians and shoppers. There was little reason to visit the once-bustling heart of the city.

Meek reminded me that Waco also lost two economic mainstays in the years following the tornado: James Connally Air Force

Base and General Tire and Rubber Company. Losing "the rubber plant," as we called it, cost the city 1,400 jobs and an annual payroll of $42 million. Those figures come from a *Waco Tribune-Herald* editorial that compared the loss of the plant "only to Baylor University pulling up stakes."

And then a storm of another sort hit the city. For fifty-one days in early 1993 a "sinful messiah"—to use the *Tribune-Herald's* description of David Koresh—and his followers held off a combined army of some seven hundred ATF and FBI agents, Texas Rangers and DPS troopers, National Guard units, and local law enforcement surrounding their Branch Davidian compound. On April 19 the whole world was watching when army tanks advanced on the building and it burst into flame. Seventy-six men, women, and children died (including four ATF agents on the first day of the siege). Although the compound was ten miles out of town, "Waco" became shorthand for a deadly mix of religious fanaticism, federal government overreach, and preventable tragedy.

My cousin Jim Holley, a Merrill Lynch executive and lifelong Wacoan, joined us for lunch. "Whenever I went somewhere and told people where I was from, that's the first thing they'd ask about," he said. "Branch Davidian."

Waco was snakebit. On May 17, 2015, a shootout erupted at a Twin Peaks restaurant where more than two hundred members of the Bandidos and other motorcycle gangs had gathered for peace talks. Nine were killed, eighteen others were wounded or injured, and 177 were arrested.

The young mayor interrupted the old Wacoans' tales of woe. The turnaround began, he told us, with his alma mater. Baylor's $266 million McLane Stadium, a spectacular glass-and-brick edifice on the Brazos River, turned heads and prompted second looks at the city itself. Baylor Bear football and basketball success followed, including national championships.

Recently a new Baylor basketball arena went up across the river from McLane. "It's close enough to downtown," Meek said, "that after a game fans can stroll downtown and have a beer or, since this is Baptist country, a fizzy Dr Pepper."

In 2013 a likable and engaging Waco couple made their debut on HGTV with *Fixer Upper*, a reality show featuring their expertise at restoring shabby, neglected houses and transforming them into cozy, inviting places to call home. It wasn't long before the whole country knew Waco—Chip and Joanna Gaines's wholesome and inviting Waco, that is. As cousin Jim put it, "Chip and Joanna moved David Koresh to the back burner."

It's hard to exaggerate the influence the couple has had on the city, even if you're not a fan of Chip's good ol' boy goofiness or Joanna's go-to design element, shiplap. When I wrote about *Fixer Upper* a few years ago, I learned from the Waco Convention and Visitors Bureau that visitors to the city in 2013 numbered 564,205. A decade later that number has nearly quadrupled—to 1,846,988 in 2022, thanks to the Fixer Uppers. The mayor reminded me that because of the show Waco in some years has attracted more visitors than the Alamo, usually the state's most popular tourist destination.

More than a million every year are drawn to the Gaineses' Magnolia Market at the Silos, a home goods emporium on the grounds of two rusty, abandoned silos a few blocks east of downtown. As a result of what Waco calls the "Magnolia effect," more than a dozen new hotels have opened and upscale restaurants have popped up. People are living downtown in spiffy lofts and condos in venerable restored buildings. ("This is Waco?" I ask myself when I drive downtown past new construction between the Silos and Austin Avenue.)

People also are moving in, Meek said—not only spilling out of fast-growing Austin and the metroplex but also arriving from around the country. Californians in particular come to town with cash for houses like the ones Chip and Joanna transform.

The couple has moved on to a new network, partnering with HGTV parent company Discovery, but they're still rooted in Waco. The Magnolia phenomenon shows no signs of slowing down. "They're great people," the mayor said. "They represent a great quality of life."

Business and industry have also rediscovered Waco. Located halfway between two of the strongest economies in the country, the city is becoming a distribution manufacturing center. Its first billion-dollar packaging center recently began construction.

When he was elected to the city council in 2015, Meek discovered that Waco itself needed fixing up. City streets were atrocious, prompting the city council to approve $27 million in improvements and repair, up from $2.5 million the year before.

Lining many of those streets were block after block of substandard housing, the result in part of absentee-owner neglect. Decrepit houses in once-solid middle- and upper-middle-class neighborhoods gave Chip and Joanna plenty to work with. Substandard housing is still a challenge, the mayor said, as is gentrification (a product of the *Fixer Upper* phenomenon). Income disparity, a persistent part of the Waco story for as long as I can remember, also remains a problem.

"Waco is not perfect, and there are still certain challenges," Meek told me, "but there's been a lot of people for years working for this moment. We don't intend to stop."

Although Meek decided not to run for another term when his term ended, he and his wife, Lindsey, and their two children are not going anywhere. Like that Waco kid under the live oaks long ago, the kid I faintly recall, they'll continue building their city. During these heady times, the Meeks and their fellow Wacoans envision a downtown minor league baseball park, a "Great Lawn" similar to Discovery Green connecting the historic Brazos River suspension bridge to historic city hall, a new performing arts center, a Brazos River boardwalk, and more.

"I tell people all the time they need to move to Waco," the mayor said. "It's small enough that you can jump in and make a difference but big enough that it feels significant."

THE IDENTITY OF FRANKLIN W. "TEX" DIXON UNVEILED AT LAST

AUSTIN

Now that a number of years have passed, I'm assuming I'm free of the statute of limitations, which means I can reveal a long-kept secret. What I can tell you is that I used to be the famed author Franklin W. Dixon.

I'm guessing you know him (me), even though the name may not be instantly familiar. And once I explain, I would advise a Santa-style secrecy around kids or grandkids who love to read.

My own familiarity with famed writer Franklin W. Dixon goes back decades, to a morning in the mid-1950s. Mom was visiting across the fence with our next-door neighbor, Mrs. Wood, a retired teacher, who mentioned that she had several boxes of books that had belonged to her son, now grown. She wondered if the Holley boys would be interested in them. Later that day my brothers and I loaded two heavy cardboard boxes onto our wagon and hauled them home.

Inside the boxes were real books, not kids' picture books. I pulled out Robert Louis Stevenson's *Kidnapped*, a football book by Claire Bee, a book about harness racing (which I'd never heard of), and a complete series of books from the 1920s and '30s—fifteen books in all—about a teenage explorer named Don Sturdy. The author was Victor Appleton.

Young Sturdy's dad is an explorer too, but in the first few books of the series he's missing, maybe even dead, so Don gets to accompany his explorer uncles on exotic and inevitably dangerous trips around the world. With their lurid covers and detailed illustrations scattered inside, I devoured them all—*Don Sturdy with the Big Snake Hunters: or, Lost in the Jungles of the Amazon, Don Sturdy in the Tombs of Gold: or, The Old Egyptian's Great Secret*, and my favorite, *Don Sturdy Captured by Head Hunters: or, Adrift in the Wilds of Borneo*. That's the one where Don and his uncles end up in large pots over a boiling fire, soon to be dinner for Borneo's head-hunting cannibals.

I loved those books and have lugged them around through move after move all these years. (I also lug around a guilty conscience about my mom having to vacuum around my bare feet one morning while I sat in the living room engrossed in *Don Sturdy among the Gorillas: or, Adrift in the Great Jungle*.)

Also in one of the boxes was another, better-known series about teenage amateur detectives. The Hardy Boys, Joe and Frank, race around Bayport, New York, in their roadster (whatever that was) and, with their pal Chet, invariably manage to solve the case before the cops can get their heads around it. I liked them almost as much as Don Sturdy. The Hardy Boys author, then and now, is Franklin W. Dixon.

Years later I was trying to cobble together a freelance career while working on a book. My agent's wife suggested that I contact her friend, a Simon & Schuster editor of the long-running Hardy Boys series.

The editor let me in on the secret. Dixon had been the Hardy Boys author from the beginning, in 1929, but he has never existed. Dixon, along with Victor Appleton, Carolyn Keene (the Nancy

Drew writer), and dozens of other "authors," were pseudonyms concocted by Edward Stratemeyer, a prolific publisher of fiction for children and teens, all of it produced by ghostwriters through the years.

The editor explained that I too could be Franklin W. Dixon if I agreed not to divulge the Dixon secret—and if I adhered to the Hardy Boys "bible." For example, Joe and older brother Frank can solve all kinds of crimes as long as they don't involve drugs. The boys like girls and might indulge in a bit of harmless ogling, hand-holding, maybe even a kiss, but certainly nothing more ardent. And every chapter except the last has to end in a cliffhanger.

Adhering to the old saw about writing what you know, I used Texas every chance I got. In *Illegal Procedure*, for example, young Joe goes undercover with the NFL's San Diego Sharks to expose a steroid scandal. (I had to get special dispensation to write about steroids.) The reason no one in the pro ranks has ever heard of Joe Hardy is that he was a speedy, sure-handed receiver at a teachers' college in far West Texas, but the school dropped football after his junior year. The Sharks signed him as a free agent, and, as the cover blurb promises, "The blitz is on, and if the Hardys don't come up with a few trick plays of their own, they could face sudden death!"

In *Moment of Truth*, the boys flee the winter cold of Bayport and head to South Padre. Renting surfboards on the beach one sunny morning, they meet Rosa Galvan, a dark-haired beauty from Matamoros. ("That's not a girl, Joe," Frank said. "That's a goddess.") She invites them to her matador brother Rigo's very first bullfight the next Sunday. (Rosa, by the way, was based on a young woman at the Matamoros VW dealership who arranged for me to get my broken-down van back across the river many years ago.)

Hemingway himself would have been proud of the handsome youngster's grace under pressure in the ring. The crowd goes wild. As Rigo—known as El Puma—basks in the adulation, a black helicopter looms over the arena. Must be a TV news chopper, Joe says to Frank—until camouflage-clad gunmen leap out and snare the bullfighter. As the chopper lifts off with Rigo in tow, the downdraft ruffles his red cape left lying on the sand. The Hardy Boys, with Rosa assisting, spring into action.

I had fun being Franklin W. "Tex" Dixon, even though it was a challenge to tell a gripping tale. It was hard to peel back the mystery layer by layer so my young readers would keep turning the page along with Joe and Frank.

After a couple of years my editor and I went on to new adventures, and so did the boys. Forever teenagers, they're still solving crimes. As far as I know, they've never made it back to South Padre.

A PUP BY ANY OTHER NAME

HOUSTON

One of my favorite names for a dog belongs to a brown-and-white spaniel that lives in East Montrose a couple of blocks off Taft. His name is Senator. His owners said they used to have a dog named Governor, so when a new dog came into their lives, Senator seemed appropriate. If he happens to be in the front yard when you walk by and you greet him with "Hello, Senator," he'll respond with a hearty bark. He's protective of his district.

Senator comes to mind, not because this is a barkingly raucous election year but because we have a new member of the family, a three-month-old blue heeler mix we've been calling Davis, in recognition of the town where we found the gangly, little guy—Fort Davis. We chose the name in part because we have a cat named Bo, short for Bomar Street. Bo was a feral kitten born two winters ago under our bungalow.

We gave a passing thought to naming Bo's bothersome interloper Fort, but Davis seemed just fine—until a friend during a Friday evening Zoom get-together alluded to the delicate matter of bestowing the name of the president of the Confederate States of America on a pet. (The frontier fort, the town, and the county are all named for Jefferson Davis.) I sensed from the expression on our friend's face that the name Davis was on a par with Adolf or Stalin or maybe John Wilkes Booth. That's not what we had in mind, of course, but we immediately realized we couldn't dismiss the historical reference. Particularly these days.

Jefferson Davis was a West Point graduate and slaveholding Mississippi planter who served in both the U.S. House and Senate before President Franklin Pierce named him secretary of war in 1853. Fort Davis was established on the San Antonio–El Paso Road the next year and named for the secretary. (Davis, by the way, is the man who championed the use of camels as pack animals in the great southwestern desert, including West Texas.) He was the Confederacy's one and only president from 1861 to 1865.

Texans had a thing for Davis in the decades following the war. With the collapse of the Confederacy, Davis was hightailing it to Texas before being captured in Georgia. After serving two years in prison, while plans to try him for treason came to naught, prominent Dallasites offered to buy him a house—with a yard as large as he wanted—if he would relocate. He declined.

In 1876 the newly established Agricultural and Mechanical College of Texas offered him the presidency. Writing on behalf of the school, Gov. Richard Coke urged him to come and reside "among a people who will never cease to love and honor you." Davis said no, in part because he owned a Memphis life insurance company and the $4,000 annual salary the Aggies offered would represent a financial sacrifice.

The Texas Legislature established Jeff Davis County in 1887. *The Handbook of Texas* quotes an unnamed Texas legislator who exulted, "Thank God that at last we have a Texas county named in honor of the president of the Confederacy."

Davis died in 1889, but in Texas and throughout the South the determined campaign to memorialize the Lost Cause had already begun. Rebel soldier statues were taking up positions on courthouse squares. Buildings, public schools, and thoroughfares were being named for Davis, Robert E. Lee, and other iconic symbols of southern defiance. At least ten American military installations, including Fort Hood, were named for men who fought to tear the nation asunder. (A Senate committee at last has voted to explore changing those names, despite President Donald Trump's outspoken opposition.)

Davis and other Confederate luminaries were losing their place of prominence even before the current effort to relegate them to history's shrouded basement. In 2015 the University of Texas at Austin removed a Davis statue from its high-profile position on the South Mall and placed it inside the Dolph Briscoe Center for American History. Schools throughout the South, including in Houston, have erased the Jefferson Davis name, realizing the importance of aspirational resonance for their students.

A longtime Fort Davis resident told me recently that the Jefferson Davis matter never comes up in the mountain town she loves. "We're not honoring him with the name," she said. "Nobody's walking around dressed like Jefferson Davis at the fort."

Back to Davis the dog. Even before the Zoom meeting, we considered other names—Ranger or Cowboy or Chisos (alluding to his Big Bend origins) or Trace (our current street). Our Marathon neighbor Russ Tidwell suggested Sully, for Sul Ross State University in nearby Alpine. It was a tongue-in-cheek suggestion since Russ knows that monuments to the old Texas Ranger, Indian-fighting rescuer of the didn't-want-to-be-rescued Cynthia Ann Parker, Confederate Army general, Texas governor, and Texas A&M president may soon meet the fate of his Confederate cohorts. Aggies, including Aggie football players, are marching.

Obviously a rose is a rose is a rose (or a dog is a dog is a dog), and yet a name can be a weighty matter. Think about the decades-long insult of Dowling Street (now Emancipation Avenue) or a Missouri City residential street named after the founder of the Ku Klux Klan. While our pup was already responding to the name after a couple of weeks of hearing it (particularly when he heard the simultaneous rustle of the dog food bag), we felt a lingering regret about the selection.

To me, the lively fellow who loped after balls in the backyard sat on command after a few days and tirelessly tried to befriend Bo has nothing to do with a traitorous Confederate president. Our Davis represented the ruggedly beautiful Davis Mountains that rise up behind the shelter where the pup spent his first few weeks. The name recalled the two chattering roadrunners that scurried back and forth across the open field within a few yards of where I socially distanced while waiting for his release into our care. The name reminded me of the good people of one of my favorite Texas towns.

And yet, can a distinction be drawn between a good place and the troubling reverberations of history? Sooner rather than later, I suspect, that's likely to be an issue for the people of Jeff Davis County.

It's not going to be an issue for the dog, however. We made our decision about a name change the same day the *New York Times* featured a graffiti-splattered statue of Jefferson Davis lying face down on a Richmond, Virginia, street. We realized that about half the time, without really thinking about it, we called the little guy Buddy. Buddy's not all that original, but our flop-eared, long-legged pal doesn't mind. His nickname sort of trips off the tongue in a way that Davis doesn't.

"Hey, Buddy," I called this morning, "let's go for a walk!" Tail wagging, he was right behind me as I headed out the door. Davis he may have been, but Buddy's what he is to us. Buddy Holley, if you will.

ACKNOWLEDGMENTS

Thanks to all my fellow Texans who share their stories, suggest topics, and read my columns, often responding with comments. They've been the lifeblood of the Native Texan column. Thanks also to Jennifer Radcliffe, my longtime *Houston Chronicle* editor, and to Tom Payton and Burgin Streetman, my editors at Trinity University Press. Thanks to daughter Kate Holley for her whimsical illustrations. Finally, thanks to Laura Tolley, my wife, who indulges my Lone Star enthusiasms (despite being a native New Mexican) and tolerates my absentmindedness when I have a column on the brain.

JOE HOLLEY has been the Native Texan columnist for the *Houston Chronicle* since 2013 and an editorial writer for the paper since 2012. A native Texan himself—from Waco—he has also been an editorial page editor in San Diego, California, a contributor to *Texas Monthly*, a speechwriter for Gov. Ann Richards, and a staff writer for the *Washington Post*. He was a Pulitzer Prize finalist in 2017 and 2023 and a 2022 Pulitzer Prize winner as part of the *Houston Chronicle* team that produced a series of editorials debunking the "Big Lie" of voter fraud and examining Texas's long history of voter suppression. He is the author of seven books, including *Hometown Texas, Hurricane Season: The Unforgettable Story of the Houston Astros and the Resilience of a City*, and *Sutherland Springs: God, Guns, and a Small Texas Town,* which received the 2021 Texas Institute of Letters Carr P. Collins Award. He lives in Austin, Texas.

Printed in the USA
CPSIA information can be obtained
at www.ICGtesting.com
JSHW042140080624
64462JS00003B/3

9 781595 349453